On Beauty

The Eranos Lectures Series

ON BEAUTY

Herbert Read
Beauty and the Beast

A. Hilary Armstrong
The Divine Enhancement of Earthly Beauties
The Hellenic and Platonic Tradition

Spring Publications, Inc.
Dallas, Texas

Eranos Lectures 6

First Spring Publications printing 1987

Published by Spring Publications, Inc.; P.O. Box 222069; Dallas, Texas 75222
Printed in the United States of America

Cover design and production by Maribeth Lipscomb and Patricia Mora

International Distributors
Spring; Postfach; 8800 Thalwil; Switzerland.
Japan Spring Sha, Inc.; 1–2–4, Nishisakaidani-Cho; Ohharano, Nishikyo-Ku; Kyoto, 610–11, Japan.
Element Books Ltd; Longmead; Shaftesbury Dorset SP7 8PL; England.

Library of Congress Cataloging-in-Publication Data
On beauty.
(The Eranos lectures series, ISSN 0743–586X ; 6)
Two lectures presented at the Eranos Conference
in Ascona, Switzerland in 1961 and 1984 respectively.
Includes bibliographical references.
Contents: Beauty and the beast / Herbert Read --
The divine enhancement of earthly beauties : the
hellenic and platonic tradition / A. Hilary Armstrong.
1. Aesthetics.   I. Read, Herbert. Beauty and the
beast.   II. Armstrong, A. H. (Arthur Hilary).
Divine enhancement of earthly beauties.   III. Title.
IV. Series: Eranos lectures ; 6.
BH39.05   1987   111'.85   87–20672
ISBN 0-88214-406-5

Eranos Lectures series: ISSN 0743–586X

Acknowledgments
"Beauty and the Beast" was a lecture presented originally at the 1961 Eranos Conference in Ascona, Switzerland, and appeared in the *Eranos Yearbook* 30–1961 (Ascona: Eranos Foundation), pp. 175–210. It is published here with the kind permission of the Eranos Foundation in agreement with the heirs of Herbert Read. "The Divine Enhancement of Earthly Beauties" was a lecture presented originally at the 1984 Eranos Conference in Ascona, Switzerland, and appeared in *Eranos Yearbook* 53–1984 (Ascona: Eranos Foundation), pp. 49–81. It is published here with the kind permission of the Eranos Foundation in agreement with the author.

Herbert Read
Beauty and the Beast

I.

I know nothing sublime which is
not some modification of power.
BURKE

"Esthetics bores me, doesn't interest me at all", declares one of the most significant of modern painters. "The slightest intervention of esthetics obstructs for me the efficiency of functioning and spoils the sauce. That is why I try to reject from my works all that could have the smell of esthetics. People with a short-sighted view have concluded from this that I enjoy painting ugly objects. Not at all! I don't worry about their being ugly or beautiful; furthermore these terms are meaningless for me; I even have the conviction that they are meaningless for everybody; I don't believe that these notions of ugliness or beauty have the slightest foundation: they are illusions[1]."

Such is the annihilating challenge which M. Jean Dubuffet hurls at our traditional concepts of beauty and ugliness. In this paper I propose to ask whether these concepts are indeed meaningless, or whether we can give them new meanings in conformity with the work of an artist like Dubuffet, who in this respect is representative of contemporary art in general.

---

[1] *New Images of Man,* by PETER SELZ, New York (Museum of Art) 1959.

One must begin with the semantic problem however boring it may be to impatient artists like Dubuffet. The whole discussion has been bedevilled by the inconsistent meanings of the words used in various languages to denote the concept of ugliness. I shall not make a pedantic survey of a confused situation, but if we confine ourselves only to the main division between the Nordic languages and the Mediterranean languages, we find a difference of connotation which makes any direct transfer of the terminology inexact and misleading. The words in the Romance languages derive from the Teutonic root *laipo-* (cf. French *laideur*, Italian *laido*) or the Latin *brutus* (cf. French *brut*, Italian *brutto*) and the original meaning of these words is dull, stupid, senseless—in general the characteristics of animals as compared with rational human beings. Incidentally, the kind of painting practised by Dubuffet is often called in French "l'art brut". The Nordic words for ugliness have a very different derivation and connotation: the German *häßlich* is the same root as *hassen,* to hate; whereas the English *ugly* comes from the Middle English *uggen,* or Old Norse *ugga,* fear, or *uggligr,* causing fear, dreadful, terrible.

In Aristotle's *Poetics* and onward through Longinus and Augustine down to the medieval scholastics, the philosophers of the Italian Renaissance and those of the Enlightenment, beauty is conceived as an excellence in the proportion of things: what is not beautiful is what is without perfection of form, or deformed, for which we have the Latin word *turpis*. If we had wanted a word of Latin derivation to describe the contrary of beauty, it should have been "turpitude". "Loathliness" is a possible alternative, and is of the same derivation as the French *laideur* and the Italian *laidezza*. In Scotland and the North of England we have the cognate word "laidly"—the Laily Worm of the ballad:

> I was bat seven year alld
> Fan my mider she did dee,
> My father marred the ae warst woman
> The wardle did ever see.

> For she has made me the laily worm
> That lays att the fitt of the tree,
> An o my sister Messry
> The machrel of the sea.

The father in the ballad discovers his wife's deception and the laily worm is transformed by three strokes of a silver wand into "the bravest knight Your eyes did ever see", and on the blowing of a small horn the machrel turn into his sister Messry once more. The precise meaning of the word "laily" or "laidly" is given when the fish exclaim:

> Ye shaped me ance an unshemly shape
> An ye's never mare shape me.

So we get the same meaning for "laidly" in English as *laid* has in French: it is a question of form, of deformity, of unshapeliness. This was the original Greek conception of ugliness—the quality of grotesqueness, something misshapen, defective, but not necessarily unaesthetic[2].

Ugliness in English has always meant something much more positive than that—some quality that causes fear, dread, terror, pain. So when an English philosopher of the Enlightenment like Edmund Burke, in his *Enquiry into the Origin of our Ideas of the Sublime and Beautiful,* comes to deal with the nature of *Ugliness,* he is compelled to make a distinction which illustrates the confusion inherent in the use of the word as the opposite of beauty:

"But though ugliness be the opposite to beauty, it is not the opposite to proportion and fitness. For it is possible that a thing may be very ugly with any proportions, and with a perfect fitness to any uses. Ugliness I imagine likewise to be consistent enough with an idea of the sublime.

---

[2] ARISTOTLE (*Poetics* V, i) describes the comic (τὸ γελοῖον) as a part (subdivision) of the ugly (τὸ αἰσχρον). The comic mask, he says, "is something ugly and misshapen without implying pain".

But I would by no means insinuate that ugliness of itself is a sublime idea, unless united with such qualities as excite a strong terror[3]."

Burke's *Enquiry* is a fascinating document in the history of ideas, the arena in which the Greek and the Teutonic concepts of ugliness meet and are reconciled in the idea of the sublime. "Sublime" itself is the reconciling word, and is an ambiguous rendering of Longinus's Greek word *hypsos,* which means no more than height or elevation. John Hall, the first English translator of Longinus's treatise (1652), gave it the title *On the Height of Eloquence.* "The Sublime", as Allen Tate in his illuminating essay on Longinus has said, "carries with it the accretions of Boileau and the English eighteenth century, and the different meanings contributed later by Burke and Kant, which are far removed from anything that I have been able to find in this third—(or is it first—) century treatise". It is true that Longinus, in his desire to indicate the effect of a heightened style, uses dramatic expressions—the sublime, he suggests, pierces everything "like a flash of lightning"; and there is his insistence, so welcome to the romantic critic, that some elements of style "depend upon nature alone"—or as Allen Tate interprets Longinus at this point, "stylistic autonomy is a delusion, because style comes into existence only as it discovers the subject; and conversely the subject exists only after it is formed by the style". This, according to Professor Tate, is Longinus's primary insight, and it is one of which Burke made full use[4].

But Burke, as I must now insist, invests the concept of the sublime with qualities that were far from the mind of Longinus. It would not have occurred to Longinus to make a distinction between the beautiful and the sublime—the whole point of his treatise is to insist that whether

---

[3] My quotations are from the second edition, edited with an Introduction and Notes by J. T. BOULTON, London (Routledge and Kegan Paul) 1958.

[4] ALLEN TATE, *Longinus,* "Lectures in Criticism", New York (Bollingen Series), 1949, pp. 43–70. For the influence of Longinus on English criticism see *Longinus and English Criticism,* by T. R. HENN, Cambridge 1934.

by instinct or design, what is excellent in art (and therefore uncommon) is a heightening, an elevation, an intensification of the commonplace. There is ecstasy, but no strangeness, no terror—indeed, ". . . the sublime is often found where there is no emotion". Far different is Burke's theory, which I will quote in his own summary:

"On closing this general view of beauty, it naturally occurs, that we should compare it with the sublime; and in this comparison there appears a remarkable contrast. For sublime objects are vast in their dimensions, beautiful ones comparatively small; beauty should be smooth, and polished; the great rugged and negligent; beauty should shun the right line, yet deviate from it insensibly; the great in many cases loves the right line, and when it deviates, it often makes a strong deviation; beauty should not be obscure; the great ought to be dark and gloomy; beauty should be light and delicate; the great ought to be solid, and even massive. They are indeed ideas of a very different nature, one being founded on pain, the other on pleasure; and however they may vary afterwards from the direct nature of their causes, yet these causes keep up an eternal distinction between them, a distinction never to be forgotten by any whose business it is to affect the passions[5]."

Vast, rugged, deviating, dark, gloomy and massive—how did Burke visualize such objects of terror and how did he explain their aesthetic effects? Burke, as indeed all philosophers of art before our time, took it for granted that the main principle of art was *mimesis*—that art made its effect by the depiction of objects or events. The examples he gives of the sublime are therefore drawn from nature rather than from literature or the plastic arts: serpents and poisonous animals are capable of raising ideas of the sublime; so is the ocean; darkness and obscurity, and here Burke gives an example from Milton, his description of the King of terrors in *Paradise Lost:*

---

[5] Op. cit., p. 124.

> The other shape,
> If shape it might be call'd that shape had none
> Distinguishable in member, joynt, or limb,
> Or substance might be call'd that shadow seem'd,
> For each seem'd either; black it stood as Night,
> Fierce as ten Furies, terrible as Hell,
> And shook a dreadful Dart; what seem'd his head
> The likeness of a Kingly Crown had on.

"In this description", says Burke, "all is dark, uncertain, confused, terrible and sublime to the last degree."

Since terror is increased by obscurity, it is better conveyed by poetry than by painting, for in painting the images tend to be too precise. Milton is quoted again—the famous portrait of Satan from Book I of *Paradise Lost;* and Burke points out that all the images in this poetical picture—a tower, an archangel, the sun rising through mists, or in an eclipse, the ruin of monarchs and the revolution of kingdoms—affect us because they are crowded and confused. But painting, Burke then admits with an air of regret, is dependent on the images it presents, and for the most part these are necessarily precise. He would not have felt the same about the images of Picasso or Dubuffet.

As a supreme example of sublimity Burke gives a passage in the *Book of Job,* where the sublimity "is principally due to the terrible uncertainty of the thing described":

> In thoughts from the visions of the night, when deep
> sleep falleth on men,
> Fear came upon me, and trembling, which made all my
> bones to shake.
> Then a spirit passed before my face; the hair of my
> flesh stood up:
> It stood still, but I could not discern the form thereof;
> an image was before mine eyes, there was silence, and I
> heard a voice saying,
> Shall mortal man be more just than God?

And he asks, quite aptly, what painting could possibly rival this vision wrapt up in the shades of its own incomprehensible darkness. Even those designs of the temptations of St. Anthony, "which I have chanced to meet", he adds, "were rather a sort of odd wild grotesques, than anything capable of producing a serious passion".

Burke quotes other examples of sublimity from the *Book of Job*—the horse whose neck is clothed in thunder, the wild ass whose house is the wilderness, the unicorn and the leviathan—wherever we look upon power, there we find that terror and sublimity are concomitant. But this is not all—all privations are terrible, Vacuity, Darkness, Solitude and Silence. Greatness of dimension, infinity, succession and uniformity which Burke called "the artificial infinite" (he gives the aisles in many of our old cathedrals as an example), sheer magnitude and difficulty (here Stonehenge is given as an example, where "the rudeness of the work increases this cause of *grandeur,* as it excludes the idea of art, and contrivance"), magnificence (Shakespeare's description of the King's army in *Henry IV,* Part I), light, or rather excessive brightness (Milton's "Dark with excessive bright"), certain colours (not soft or cheerful, but sad and fuscous colours, as black, or brown, or deep purple), the noise of vast cataracts, raging storms, thunder or artillery, the shouting of multitudes; a sudden beginning or sudden cessation of sound; and, almost opposite to this, low, tremulous, intermitting sounds; the cries of animals in pain or danger; cups of bitterness, poisonous exhalations —little more need be added to the catalogue, for in conclusion Burke suggests that "the idea of bodily pain, in all the modes and degrees of labour, pain, anguish, torment, is productive of the sublime; and nothing else in this sense can produce it". But he adds this acute psychological observation: that the sublime is an idea belonging to self-preservation. The passions which belong to self-preservation are painful when their causes immediately affect us; are delightful (though not pleasurable—Burke distinguishes sharply between delight and pleasure) when we have an idea of pain or danger without being actually involved in the circumstances. That is to say: vicarious ideas of pain, sickness and death fill the mind with strong emotions of horror: they intensify our awareness of life; whereas normal life and health, by simple enjoyment, make no such impression.

We begin to see how the idea of ugliness can be reconciled, not with the pleasure of beauty, but with the delights of sublimity. Ugliness is the physical aspect of certain objects of terror, objects which inspire fear or terror if they are real, but delight if they are counterfeit.

Why should we delight in representations of pain, sickness or death, which fill the mind with horror? The conventional explanation, that the mind is thrilled by an experience which it *knows* to be unreal, is not very convincing. If the mind is constantly aware of the unreality of the enactment, it will remain in a state of ambiguity, and though ambiguity is now a fully recognized aesthetic factor[6], it is not confined to representations of pain, sickness or death: it can be present in any process of artistic creation and communication. The explanation becomes a little more convincing when it is said that the mind *discovers* the representation that has momentarily inspired fear to be unreal. It is then assumed that the spectator is at first misled into assuming that the enactment of a terrible tragedy is a real event in which he is participating, and is then delighted to discover that it was all pretence. We experience a similar feeling of delight when we awake from a terrifying nightmare and slowly realize that it was all a dream, and that our fears are unnecessary.

We are reminded of Aristotle's theory of *catharsis*, and it may be that modern psychology has not advanced much beyond Aristotle. I do not wish to weary you with still another discussion of catharsis, but it is perhaps worth emphasizing that Aristotle always insists on the necessity,

---

[6] Cf. WILLIAM EMPSON, *The Seven Types of Ambiguity,* London 1931; ERNST KRIS and ABRAHAM KAPLAN, *Aesthetic Ambiguity*, in: *Psycho-analytical Explorations in Art*, New York 1952, ch. 10.

not only of pity, but also of fear as an element in effective tragedy. When he comes to describe what kind of incidents produce an effect of fear, he makes some extremely interesting qualifications. For example, neither pity nor fear is inspired when an enemy kills his enemy, when the antagonists are strangers to one another. But the situation is very different if such incidents occur between near kinsmen, as when a brother kills a brother, or a son his father; and it is better still, more horrible, more terrifying, if the deed is done in ignorance and the kinship of the person killed is then revealed. One should perhaps note that in this connection Aristotle distinguishes between fear and disgust. Disgust is not tragic, not aesthetic, not sublime.

Sublimity, the elevation of the mind, ought to be the principal end of all our studies, as Burke says, but he recognizes that we cannot go far in these studies without asking questions about the mind itself. In a passage which is one of the earliest anticipations of a theory of the unconscious[7], Burke suggests that "a consideration of the rationale of our passions seems to me very necessary for all who would affect them upon solid and sure principles. It is not enough to know them in general; to affect them after a delicate manner, or to judge properly of any work designed to affect them, we should know the exact boundaries of their several jurisdictions; we should pursue them through all their variety of operations, and pierce into the inmost, and what might appear inaccessible parts of our nature,

Quod latet arcana non enarrabile fibra"

—A line from Persius's *Satires* (V, 29) which might be taken as a still earlier anticipation of the Freudian unconscious.

The full consideration of our subject will inevitably lead us to the unconscious, but before we try to pierce its "arcana fibra", I would like to describe in more detail the place which ugliness in its fearsome

---

[7] Part I, section XIX, "The Conclusion".

aspects has occupied in the art of the past. I must first deal with the
paradox inherent in all this discussion of ugliness. The artist has a certain power of transfiguration. That is to say, he may take an object that
is inherently ugly or disgusting—the flayed carcase of an ox, the guil-
lotined head of a criminal, the tortured body of a martyred saint, a
crippled idiot or a loathsome reptile, and by painting these subjects with
loving care, by giving them aesthetic values of colour and composition,
he creates a "distance" between the reality and our perception which in
effect transforms the ugly object into a beautiful work of art. Consider
for a moment Grünewald's Isenheim altarpiece, the prototype for all
such transfigurations. Here is no deformation, no dehumanisation: on
the contrary, a relentless objectivity or realism. If it is felt that we cannot
exclude from our contemplation of such a subject religious emotions
which vitally affect our aesthetic responses, then we may substitute
Rembrandt's "Flayed Ox"—the aesthetic considerations are identical.
In all such works of art we shall find the operation of certain modalities
of expression which have the effect of sublimating the object represented.
In Aristotle such modalities are called "poetic diction", and in tragedy
we mean that certain subjects or events may be described in verse which
could not be described in prose—I have already quoted Burke's examples from *Paradise Lost* and *The Book of Job*. A corresponding process
takes place in painting: that is to say, the object, the crucified body of
Christ or the flayed ox, is painted with such skill and such delicacy, that
we are lost in admiration of the manner, and do not react to the horror
of the object itself. The art of the artist by this means creates an aesthetic
"distance" between the crude reality and our organs of perception.

By definition all works of art, whether literary or plastic or musical,
must embody an aesthetic principle, and it may be that this factor of
"distance" is always present in a work of art to a greater or lesser degree.
But the distinction I want to make is one between works of art which
depict the ugly object almost, one might say, with love, accept it in its

hideous reality and lift it on to a plane of acceptance; and those works of art which are a deformation of reality, a caricature, grotesque, perverse, in every sense defamatory, and which we accept, if we accept at all, as afflictions, as corrections, as punishments, as a protest. In such cases the deformation is not in the object itself but in the artist's vision of it. In one case the artist accepts the ugliness he finds in nature and redeems it by his art; in the other case the artist by his art creates an ugliness that does not exist in nature, but which nevertheless has positive qualities that fill us with emotions of terror and delight. That ugliness exists in nature and causes us aesthetic displeasure is a remarkable fact but not one which need concern us at the moment. Far more puzzling is the fact that ugliness is deliberately created and seems to satisfy some social or psychological need. What is the nature of its attractiveness? Why are we fascinated by what is at the same time fearful?

First let me dismiss the assumption, frequently found in traditional aesthetics, that aesthetically speaking such questions are non-sensical. "All art", asserted one of the most intelligent of English philosophers of art, "except that of children, savages, ignoramuses and extreme innovators, invariably avoids ugly shapes and seeks for beautiful ones; *but art does this while pursuing all manner of different aims*[8]." The different aims include "the awakening, intensifying or maintaining of definite emotional states", but even these "aids to devotion", as they are called, must presumably avoid ugly shapes. It is simply not true, and to make an exception of "children, savages, ignoramuses and extreme innovators" is to exclude a vast range of aesthetic experience. Vernon Lee wrote these words in 1912 or 1913, when the art of savages, so called, had already made a decisive contribution to the foundations of modern art. The tendency that began with Picasso's *Demoiselles d'Avignon* of 1907 was based on a conscious acceptance of ugliness as a positive factor

---

[8] VERNON LEE, *The Beautiful* (Cambridge 1913), p. 99.

in aesthetic experience. The whole course of the modern movement
during the past half-century is almost a reversal of the academic tradition in aesthetics so ably expounded by Vernon Lee (and she bases
herself on Fechner, Semper, Lipps, Wundt, and the other founders of
this tradition)—indeed we might say that modern art invariably avoids
beautiful shapes and seeks for ugly ones. But it is none the less art, and
that is the paradox we have to explain.

I must not, however, allow the assumption that it is the art of the past
fifty years, and that art alone, which seeks its effects through ugly shapes.
Ugliness has always been present in art, from prehistoric times and
throughout all subsequent periods. What could be uglier than the
Venuses of Laussel and Willendorf, representative images from the
Palaeolithic period? Only, perhaps, the nudes of Rouault or Beckmann.
Mesopotamian art, Egyptian art, Cycladic art, Chinese art, Etruscan art,
Gothic art, Renaissance art—in all these epochs we find, not merely
depictions of natural ugliness, but wilful deformations of natural objects
that are not ugly in themselves. And all this is apart from the art of so-
called savage peoples, the tribal art of Africa and Oceania, that contra-
dicts all the canons of beauty which have predominated in our own
civilization.

Before seeking the explanation of this paradox, let me give some specific instances. I have already mentioned the palaeolithic Venuses. They
are not all ugly—the Venus of Lespugue has had the beauty treatment,
is "stylised", as we say, and conforms to what Vernon Lee calls "the
aesthetic imperative". The ugly palaeolithic Venuses may be more or
less realistic representations of the shapes of pregnant palaeolithic
women—similar shapes can be found among the women of primitive
tribes in Australia or Africa today. Such carved images were cult objects, and their original purpose was presumably not aesthetic. But we
ourselves treat them as rare examples of the art of prehistoric man: we
classify them as works of art, ugly as they are.

The same is generally true of a vast number of cult objects characteristic of early civilizations throughout the Near and Far East—I refer in particular to the sculpture and clay figurines of Mesopotamia. There is a great variety of style in these civilizations of the third and second millenia B.C., but one can distinguish between two types which we might call secular and sacred. The secular objects, portraits of kings and officials, representations of animals, can easily be assimilated to our ideal of beauty. But the sacred objects, figures of gods and goddesses, fertility amulets, objects used in burial rites, etc., are inspired by no such ideal. Their distortions are designed to strike terror or awe into the beholder. Describing a group of statues with preternaturally large eyes found at Tell Asmar and now in the Baghdad Museum, Professor André Parrot, in his recent book on *Sumer,* suggests that they may represent a king and queen and high dignitaries of the city, praying to the gods, in particular to those who grant fertility and fecundity to the region. "Their lips are shut, but the tenseness of the bodies and the keen stare of their eyes are more eloquent than words. From this petrified group there emanates something of that awe and apprehension which historians of religion have described in analysing the sensations primitive man experiences in the presence of the numinous[9]."

Awe and apprehension are usually evoked by supernatural powers and phenomena, but how is it possible that such feelings can be aroused by human artifacts? I find a difficulty here which art historians tend to ignore. In discussing one of these same figures sometimes called the God Abu, André Malraux, in his introduction to Professor Parrot's book, suggests that such statues "made the sacred beings present in the spectator's emotion, as their ideograms made them present in his mind. ... *The God Abu* does not suggest a person who might look like him; such a person is unthinkable. Nor does the company of figures attending him

---

[9] *Sumer,* by ANDRÉ PARROT, Paris and London 1960, p. 106.

suggest a *human* assemblage invested with an aura of the sacred, it is sacred in respect of all that differentiates it from any human assemblage. For we now know better than to attribute to inexpertness the flagrant disproportion between the tiny hands of the goddess of Tell Asmar and her enormous eyes. During five centuries those strange eyes, with their corneas of bone and eyelids in bitumen, reappear again and again. In making them, the aim of the Sumerian sculptor was not to express himself as an individual; they are means to creation in the fullest sense, since the sculptor was releasing the human figure from man's estate and allying it with the figures of the gods; illuminating a human visage with a gleam of the divine[10]."

I find it difficult to associate such a transcendental experience with the humble craftsmanship of these objects. It is even difficult to use such language in relation to the work of great geniuses like Michelangelo and Rembrandt. I do not attribute to art a social function less lofty than that which Malraux attributes to it; but when he describes this function as "the imposition on the visible of a sacred order, as it were a cosmic orchestration, that both orientates men's veneration and frees it from the chaos of appearances", then I must ask: from where does the craftsman get his sacred order, who teaches him the elements of a cosmic orchestration? M. Malraux merely refers us to a communion with the gods. So transcendent is the purpose of art that the artist is unaware of it "as the saint is unaware of his sainthood".

I should be in M. Malraux's good company if I were to pass rapidly from Sumer to Egypt, from Egypt to Greece, from Greece to China and Persia, and so through all the many halls in his imaginary museum, dividing the sacred from the secular, beauty from ugliness. But M. Malraux has not used the word "ugly", and resorts rather to such periphrases as "the sacred, rendered in a vein of fantasy". To force the

---

[10] Op. cit., p. xxv.

issue I must maintain that if the Adam of Michelangelo is beautiful, if the Hermes of Praxiteles is beautiful, then in the meaning that tradition has given to the word, the god and goddess Abu are ugly, and we are therefore involved in attributing ugliness to the sacred order.

There is, of course, the Manichaean solution to this dilemma. Evil may be as transcendent as holiness, and corresponding to the beauty of holiness we would then naturally assume the existence of the ugliness of evil. That is really the assumption behind the ugliness of Satan in Christian art—the ugliness of all demonology, the iconography of Hell. All religions naturally fall into this antinomial pattern. But before accepting this easy solution of the problem—and it is no solution, but only a convenient statement of it— let us glance in one or two directions where the pattern is not so symmetrical. I find two such disturbing perspectives—one in the realm which for want of a better word we call "primitive" art; the other in the realm which also for want of a better word we call "modern" art.

In considering primitive art we must be particularly careful of verbal equivocation. There are rare exceptions, such as the wonderful bronze heads from Ife and Benin, to which we can legitimately apply our concept of beauty, and there may have been historical influences to account for this. But apart from such rare exceptions, this primitive world of art is dominated by terror and fear, and every work of art is (again in our sense of the word) sublimely ugly. There is no antinomy in this world, no antithesis of good and evil, of god and the devil, of Ormuzd and Ahriman. There are various forces immanent and all pervasive.

In African philosophy all being, all essence, in whatever form it is conceived, is conceived not as substance but as force. "Man is a force, all things are forces, place and time are forces and the 'modalities' are forces. Man and woman ... dog and stone ... east and yesterday ... beauty and laughter ... are forces and as such are related to one another[11]." The artist is the man who can control these forces and give them formal existence. The work of art is magical because it is an embodiment of the sublime forces that determine all being.

A belief in these forces inspires the whole complex of primitive art. All its formal conventions and modes of representation are conceived in awe and express a desire to tap the sources of a supreme spiritual power.

Let me quote one other authority, but I think the best, for this generalization: Mr. William Fagg, of the Department of Ethnography, the British Museum. I do so advisedly, because in the work from which I am to quote he warns us that "most of those who have written from an aesthetic point of view on African sculpture have succeeded only in interposing an opaque screen of largely irrelevant verbiage between it and the student[12]". Mr. Fagg, in the work in question, who gives a very comprehensive survey of all the varieties of African sculpture, writes of "the doctrine of force which unites in a single system the three concepts (each having its appropriate art forms) of the worship of gods and spirits, the cult of the ancestors, and the direct harnessing of energy through charms and fetishes". This is how he describes this informing force:

"It is probable that the most fundamental quality of African sculpture is dynamism; but in trying to apply this concept in art we have passed beyond the field of scientific evidence into one where, for the present, we must rely largely on conjecture and speculation. We know from the plentiful evidence collected by missionaries and anthropologists that the life of many if not most African tribes is pervaded by this concept of

---

[11] Cf. JANHEINZ JAHN, *Muntu; an Outline of Neo-African Culture*. Trans. MARJORIE GRENE, London (Faber) 1961. Original edition Eugen-Diederichs-Verlag, 1958. Jahn bases this account of African philosophy on ALEXIS KAGAME, *La philosophie bantu-rwandaise de l'Etre*, Bruxelles 1956.

[12] *The Sculpture of Africa*. By ELIOT ELISOFON. Text by WILLIAM FAGG. London (Thames & Hudson) 1958.

dynamism (normally defined as a theory which explains the phenomena of the universe by immanent energy). It has been most explicitly described by Father Placide Tempels in his *Philosophie bantoue* (1947) on the basis of his long researches among the Baluba. ... According to Tempels, African thought is conditioned by their ontology, that is, their theory of the nature of being: for them being is a process and not a mere state, and the nature of things is thought of in terms of force or energy rather than matter; the forces of the spirit, human, animal, mineral and vegetable worlds are all constantly influencing each other, and by a proper knowledge and use of them a man may influence his own life and that of others. ... This interpretation of African belief about the nature of things accords well with what we have long known of tribal peoples in other continents, especially the concept of 'soul stuff' in South-East Asia and *mana* in Polynesia. All these peoples seem to share a belief in the desirability of increase in the broadest sense as a principal end of life, together with a corresponding fear of loss of force."

It will be realized, perhaps, that we have returned to something very near to Burke's concept of the sublime. Burke, of course, had no knowledge of Negro art, but he had a concept of nature, and of the sensationalist basis of our aesthetic reactions, which corresponds very closely to this description of African thought. Let me remind you of a few of his definitions:

"The passion caused by the great and sublime in *nature*, when those causes operate most powerfully, is Astonishment; and astonishment is that state of the soul, in which all its motions are suspended, with some degree of horror. In this case the mind is so entirely filled with its object, that it cannot entertain any other, nor by consequence reason on that object which employs it."

"There are many animals who, though far from being large, are yet capable of raising ideas of the sublime, because they are considered as objects of terror. As serpents and poisonous animals of all kinds. And to things of great dimensions, if we annex an adventitious idea of terror, they become without comparison greater. A level plain of a vast extent on land is certainly no mean idea; the prospect of such a plain may be as extensive as a prospect of the ocean; but can it ever fill the mind with anything so great as the ocean itself? This is owing to several causes, but it is owing to none more than this, that the ocean is an object of no small terror."

Burke speaks of certain animals in whom the idea of a supernatural force is inherent, and who are therefore terrifying but sublime—the bull and the horse can become sublime in this sense, whereas in the gloomy forest, and in the howling wilderness, are animals like the lion, the tiger, the panther and rhinoceros in whom the terrible and the sublime always blaze out together.

Burke gives many other examples of the all-pervasiveness of sublime forces in nature, and these forces are always associated with a sense of vastness and infinity, of fear and astonishment. He even ventures to contemplate the idea of God, and to argue that his all-pervasive force cannot be separated from the idea of infinite power, and therefore of terror. "Thus when we contemplate the Deity, his attributes and their operation, coming united on the mind, form a sort of sensible image, and as such are capable of affecting the imagination. Now, though in a just idea of the Deity, perhaps none of his attributes are (*sic*) predominant, yet to our imagination, his power is by far the most striking. Some reflection, some comparing is necessary to satisfy us of his wisdom, his justice, and his goodness; to be struck with his power, it is only necessary that we should open our eyes. But whilst we contemplate so vast an object, under the arm, as it were, of almighty power, and invested upon every side with omnipresence, we shrink into the minuteness of our own nature, and are, in a manner, annihilated before him. And though a consideration of his other attributes may relieve in some measure our apprehensions; yet no conviction of the justice with which it is exercised, nor the mercy with which it is tempered, can wholly remove the terror that naturally arises from a force which nothing can withstand ... when the prophet David contemplated the wonders of wisdom and power, which are displayed in the economy of man, he seems to be struck with a sort of divine horror, and cries out, *fearfully and wonderfully am I made!*[13]."

It may seem that I am making an improbable connection between this eighteenth-century philosopher's conception of God and the African native's conception of Nature; but I do not think so: the same all-pervasive power is conceived, capable of inspiring fear and astonishment and capable, through embodiment in sensible images, of striking terror in the beholder. "A sort of divine horror" is present in both conceptions, and I would maintain that the quality in works of art to which Burke gives the name "sublime" is identical with that to which the anthropologists give the name "dynamic energy". African sculpture, and primitive art generally, can by no means be related to our concept of beauty; I see no difficulty in relating it to this distinct concept of the sublime.

Finally, before I attempt to analyze the sources of this power in our psychological nature, in the economy of man, let me briefly refer to the same concepts in modern art.

The relation of modern art to primitive art is an historical fact: the decisive influence of African sculpture on Picasso and Braque, Brancusi and Henry Moore, has been acknowledged by the artists themselves. But apart from that specific instance, from 1889 onwards, when primitive art was first exhibited in Europe, a general assimilation of the formal qualities of African, Oceanic, American Indian, Mexican and other primitive types of art began to take place, until a point was reached when the whole of the so-called modern movement abandoned the traditional concept of beauty and moved over to this alternative concept which Burke called the sublime. One does not often think of modern art as sublime; but remembering the definitions made by Burke which I have

---

[13] Op. cit., Part Two, section v.

quoted, there can be no doubt that in its general characteristics it closely conforms to his idea of an irrational and violent experience. Again and again modern artists have disowned the concept of the beautiful. "Art", Picasso once said, "is not the application of a canon of beauty but what the instinct and the brain can conceive beyond any canon[14]." "Beauty", Henry Moore once wrote, "in the later Greek or Renaissance sense, is not the aim of my sculpture. Between beauty of expression and power of expression there is a difference of function. The first aims at pleasing the senses, the second has a spiritual vitality which for me is more moving and goes deeper than the senses[15]." In these forthright denials of beauty two of the most representative masters of the modern movement at the same time assert a positive aim that goes beyond sensuous pleasure, to affirm vitality, intensity, and that "sort of divine horror" which their works, in their extreme limits, relentlessly inspire.

In order to understand this turning away from beauty and pleasure, this frenetic deformation and disfiguration of the fair face of nature, we must turn our attention inwards, to the psyche, where all images are made and unmade, where pleasure and delight, fear and affliction, alternate in endless dialectical rhythm, like those hammers of the Cyclops described by Virgil in the *Aeneid,* a passage which Burke quotes in another context and provides this translation:

"Three rays of twisted showers, three of watery clouds, three of fire, and three of the winged southwind; then mixed they in the work terrific lightnings, and sound, and fear, and anger, with pursuing flames[16]."

---

[14] *Conversation avec Picasso* (CHRISTIAN ZERROS), "Cahiers d'Art", Paris 1935, vol. 10, no. 10, pp. 173–178.

[15] Statement in *Unit one,* edited by HERBERT READ, London 1934.

[16] *Aeneid* VIII, 429–432:

> Tres imbris torti radios, tres nubis aquosae
> Addiderant; rutili tres ignis et alitis austri;
> Fulgores nunc terrificos, sonitumque, metumque
> Miscebant operi, flammisque sequacibus iras.

Vulcan, or Hephaestus, as I have already suggested in a previous lecture, is the archetypal artist and his forged thunderbolts are deliverances of fear with which we readily associate the idea of the sublime. Significantly enough for our argument, Vulcan, deformed, lame and dishevelled, is also the archetype of ugliness.

II.

> Greek art has taught us that
> there are no truly beautiful
> surfaces without dreadful depths.
> NIETZSCHE

The story of "Beauty and the Beast", "La Belle et la Bête", was written by Madame Leprince de Beaumont, who was born at Rouen in 1711 and died near Annecy in 1780. It immediately became a very popular fairy-tale, was translated into all languages, and the name of the authoress was forgotten. On a modest scale she had given the world what Sophocles and Shakespeare and Goethe gave it—an archetypal myth. Let me recall some of the details of her story.

Once upon a time there lived a very rich merchant who had six children, three boys and three girls. Of the daughters all were beautiful, but, as in "King Lear", the two elder ones were proud and selfish; whereas the youngest one, who was called Beauty, was modest and refused all offers of marriage because she was devoted to her father.

The merchant suddenly lost all his wealth except a small house in the country, to which they retired. This reversal of fortune was very disagreeable to the two eldest daughters, but Beauty resolved to try and be happy in spite of their poverty. While her father and brothers worked on the land, she did the housework and the cooking, and in the evening she would read, or play the harpsichord, or sing at the spinning-wheel. Her sisters remained idle and discontented.

After living in poverty for a year the merchant heard that one of his ships, which he had believed lost, had returned to port laden with merchandise. The merchant set off for the port, first asking his daughters what they would like him to bring back for them. The two eldest asked for rich dresses and jewels, but Beauty asked only for a rose—"for none grows here".

When he arrived at the port the merchant found that all his goods had been distrained by his creditors, so he had to go back home as poor as when he had set out. It was only about thirty miles to his house, but he had to pass through a great wood in which he lost his way. It was snowing heavily and blowing so hard that twice he fell from his horse. Suddenly, at the end of a long cutting in the trees, he saw a bright light shining ahead of him; so he led his horse towards it and came to a great castle all lit up. There was no one about, but there was an open stable full of hay and oats upon which his hungry horse fell with avidity. He himself entered the castle and in the great hall found a fire burning and a table laden with food, and laid only for one guest. He dried himself before the fire, and waited some time, but no one appeared. Unable to resist the pangs of hunger any longer, he devoured a chicken, drank several glasses of wine and then went off in search of a bed, which he found and on which he lay down and slept.

When he awoke at ten o'clock next morning he found everything prepared for him, clean clothes and a cup of hot chocolate. Outside the snow had disappeared and the garden was bright with flowers. He went out to look for his horse, and in passing by a bed of roses suddenly remembered Beauty's request. He stooped to pick one, and at that moment there was a terrible roar, and looking up he saw a hideous beast, so horrible that he nearly fainted. "How ungrateful you are", roared the Beast. "I saved your life by taking you into my castle, and in return for my hospitality you steal my roses, which I love better than anything in the world. You must therefore die to expiate your crime and I shall give you only a quarter of an hour to make your peace with God." The poor merchant threw himself upon his knees—"My lord", he pleaded, "I did not think I would offend you so gravely by plucking a rose for one of my daughters, who had asked me to bring her one."

"I am not a lord", replied the monster, "I am a Beast. I do not like compliments. I prefer people who say what they think, and you do not move me with your flattery. But since you tell me you have some daughters, I will forgive you on condition one of them comes here willingly to die in your stead. Do not argue with me; go immediately, but before you go, swear that in three months you will return if meanwhile one of your daughters does not come to die in your place."

The merchant gave this promise and then the Beast told him to return to his chamber and fill the chest he would find there with anything that took his fancy and the Beast would have it carried to his house. He went to the room and filled the chest with gold.

The merchant then mounted his horse, which found its own way through the forest paths without difficulty. Within a few hours the good man was at home again being greeted by his excited children. To Beauty he gave the rose, saying: "Take it; it cost your father very dear." He then told them the whole story.

The elder sisters turned on Beauty with all kind of insults, but in the end Beauty, on her own insistence, returned to the castle with her father and the same welcome awaited them. When they had finished supper there was a great roar and the Beast appeared and asked Beauty if she had come of her own free will. On replying that it was so, the Beast turned to the father and told him he must return the next morning, leaving his daughter behind. They then went to bed and in the morning the father full of remorse said goodbye to his daughter.

Then begins the Beast's wooing of Beauty in this enchanted castle. Gradually Beauty was overwhelmed with sympathy for the poor Beast, because he was so kind to her, and in the end she grew accustomed to his ugliness. But when he asked her to be his wife, she could but refuse, much to the distress of the Beast. Finally she asked if she might return home to see her father, for in a magic mirror in her room she had seen that he was ill and pining. Reluctantly the Beast allowed her to go home but told her that she must return at the end of a week or he would pine away.

Beauty was then transported to her home where she rejoined her joyful father and her jealous sisters. The sisters were so envious that they plotted to keep Beauty beyond the permitted week, in the hope that the Beast would be so angry that he would then devour her. Beauty was prevailed upon to stay one more week, but on the tenth night she dreamt that she was back in the castle garden and that she saw the Beast lying prostrate on the grass.

Full of pity for the Beast, the next morning, thanks to a magic ring the Beast had given her for the purpose, she found herself back in the castle and waited for the Beast to appear. But he did not appear; so she searched everywhere in the castle, and then, remembering her dream, ran down the garden and found him lying there unconscious. His heart was still beating and she revived him by sprinkling water on his forehead. The Beast opened his eyes and told Beauty that he no longer wanted to live since she had forgotten her promise. "Oh my dear Beast, you must not die", cried Beauty, "but live and marry me. I thought that it was only friendship I felt for you, but the grief I felt when I thought you were dead made me see that I cannot live without you."

No sooner had Beauty said these words than the whole castle lit up, with fireworks and music. The Beast had disappeared and in his place she saw a Prince more beautiful than Love himself. A wicked fairy, the Prince explained, had cast a spell on him and he had to remain in the form of a Beast until a beautiful girl offered to marry him. A transformation scene follows, complete with a fairy, who says to Beauty: "Come and receive the reward for the choice you have made; you have preferred virtue to beauty and wit, and you now deserve to find all these qualities in the one you love. You will become a great queen; may your throne not destroy your virtue." The elder sisters are duly admonished, the marriage takes place in the Prince's Kingdom, and they lived a very long time in perfect happiness because their love was founded on virtue.

This story has certain parallels with other legends and fairy-tales, such as "Cinderella" and Andersen's "Ugly Duckling", but for our purpose it is the most perfect constellation of archetypal images. To begin with, we have two sets of triads, one male (the three brothers), one female (the three sisters), which for each sex may be said to represent three of the four functions of consciousness. To acquire wholeness it is necessary to discover and make conscious the fourth function, which is buried in the unconscious (represented in our fairy-tale by the great castle hidden in the woods). But this fourth function is disguised in an ugly shape and, before it can be united with the other functions, must be transformed. The symbol of transformation is "the flower of peace, the Rose that cannot wither[17]", but the rose cannot be plucked, the love cannot be consummated, until certain conditions have been fulfilled. The essential test is that ugliness itself should be spontaneously loved, and this is brought about by the kindness of the Beast, which is contrasted with the envy of Beauty's two sisters, who do everything they can to thwart the union of Beauty and the Beast.

In the story we also find certain subsidiary objects which have a symbolic value such as the chest which the father was allowed to fill with gold, and which was magically transported to his house, and the magic mirror in which, while a prisoner in the castle (the unconscious), Beauty could see her absent father. It would not serve my immediate purpose to enlarge on the significance of these symbols. What is important for

---

[17] Cf. *The Flower of Peace*, Eranos-Jahrbuch XXVII/1959, p. 318.

our present discussion is the dramatic symbolization of the four functions of consciousness.

Let me first remind you of Jung's classic description of the four functions in *The Structure and Dynamics of the Psyche*[18]:

"Consciousness is primarily an organ of orientation in a world of
outer and of inner facts. First and foremost, it establishes the fact that
something is there. I call this faculty *sensation*. By this I do not mean
the specific activity of any of the senses, but perception in general.
Another faculty interprets what is perceived; this I call *thinking*. By
means of this function, the object perceived is assimilated and its transformation into a psychic content proceeds much further than in mere
sensation. A third faculty establishes the value of the object. This function of evaluation I call *feeling*. The pain-pleasure reaction of feeling
marks the highest degree of subjectivation of the object. Feeling brings
subject and object into such a close relationship that the subject must
choose between acceptance and rejection."

(At this point let me observe how perfectly our fairy-tale illustrates
this point: it is the growth of sympathetic feeling in Beauty's concious-
ness that enables her to choose between acceptance and rejection of the
Beast.)

To continue with Jung's description: "These three functions could
be quite sufficient for orientation if the object in question were isolated
in space and time. But, in space, every object is in endless connection
with a multiplicity of other objects; and, in time, the object represents
merely a transition from a former state to a succeeding one. Most of the
spatial relationships and temporal changes are unavoidably unconscious
at the moment of orientation, and yet, in order to determine the meaning
of an object, space-time relationships are necessary. It is the fourth
faculty of consciousness, *intuition*, which makes possible, at least ap-

---

[18] *Collected Works,* vol. 8, pp. 123/24.

proximately, the determination of space-time relationships. This is a function of perception which includes subliminal factors, that is, the possible relationship to objects not appearing in the field of vision, and the possible changes, past and future, about which the object gives no clue. Intuition is an immediate awareness of relationships that could not be established by the other three functions at the moment of orientation."

The integration of the personality implies a conscious awareness and balance of all four functions. But it often happens in our psychological experience "that three of the four functions can become differentiated, i.e. conscious, while the other remains connected with the matrix, the unconscious, and is known as the 'inferior' function". It is (as Jung observes in another context) "the Achilles heel of even the most heroic consciousness; somewhere the strong man is weak, the clever man foolish, the good man bad, and the reverse is also true[19]". In our story, the beautiful man is ugly, and that is what our story is about: the transformation of ugliness into beauty, of blindness into perception, so that the four functions of consciousness can achieve perfect unity.

The function inhibited in "Beauty and the Beast" is feeling, but the story makes it clear that space-time relationships are also involved, as in most fairy-tales. They will be resolved at the moment of orientation, which is the scene of transformation.

Let us now ask why a wicked fairy has cast a spell of ugliness on a Prince "more beautiful than Love himself". The wicked fairy represents the drive that has produced a dissociation of consciousness, a complex, as we call it, and has substituted, in the field of perception, this unpleasant object, the ugly Beast. Beauty in her feminine consciousness has encountered a masculine counterpart, a hideous animus. But the father, too, is aware of the Beast's ugliness; indeed, it was the father

---

[19] *The Archetypes of the Collective Unconscious. Collected Works*, vol. 9, Part I, 237.

who first penetrated the castle, the unconscious, and found there the rose of Peace guarded by the terrifying Beast. The daughter becomes a father substitute, a daughter distinguished from her sisters by her lack of envy. This daughter is prepared to die for her father. Incidentally, in the story, it is from her father that she first receives the symbolic rose, which the Beast had allowed him to bring away from the castle.

It is tempting to interpret the Beast as the Shadow, that archetype of the dark aspects of the personality, the negative side of the psyche, but according to Jung's conception of this archetype, it is always of the same sex as the subject: it represents first and foremost the personal unconscious. The contrasexual archetype in a woman is the animus, a male principle. Why, in this fairy-tale, is it rejected: why is it ugly?

To find an explanation of this paradox I think we shall have to leave the sphere of Jungian psychology and take hints from some later developments of Freudian psychology; but first let us note that Jung does admit, parenthetically, that the father is the factor involved in the projection of the animus for the daughter, just as the mother is the factor for the son[20]. Jung also points out that these archetypes are often projected in the form of animals. But why as an ugly monster?

According to Freud, the early stages of the Oedipus conflict are dominated by sadism. They fall within a phase of development which is inaugurated by oral sadism and terminates when the ascendancy of anal sadism comes to an end[21]. In *Beyond the Pleasure Principle* Freud relates how he came to modify his earlier hypothesis of a polymorphous sexual instinct into an opposition between two kinds of instincts, one kind being directed towards an "object", the other towards the ego. Then, from further researches into the libido-development of the child in its earliest phases, it became clear that the ego is the true and original reservoir of the libido, "which is extended to the object only from this.

---

[20] Cf. *Aion*, 111.
[21] Cf. MELANIE KLEIN, *Contributions to Psycho-analysis,* London 1948, pp. 249, 269/70.

The ego took its place as one of the sexual objects and was immediately recognized as the choicest among them. Where the libido remained attached to the ego, it was termed 'narcissistic'[22]." The difference between these two kinds of instinct, which had formerly been regarded as qualitative, now had to be defined topographically, and a neurosis could then be seen as the result of a conflict between the ego and the libidinous investment of an object. The main development of Freudian psychoanalysis seems to have been an investigation of this hypothesis. Freud's own final position was based on a sharp distinction between libido and the death instinct, which he renamed Eros and Thanatos. As a further consequence of this hypothesis, Freud suggested that "object-love itself displays a second such polarity, that of love (tenderness) and hate (aggression)". A sadistic component in the sexual instinct was recognized, and as a perversion this can attain independence and dominate the sexual life of a person.

Freud pointed out that in infancy, at the oral stage of organization of the libido, amorous possession is still one and the same as annihilation of the object, and it is this aspect of psychic development that Melanie Klein took up with such fervour. Her own summary of the matter will lead us straight to the point I wish to make:

"In his book *Beyond the Pleasure Principle,* Freud put forward a theory according to which at the outset of the life of the human organism the instinct of aggression, or the death-instinct, is being opposed and bound by the libido, or life-instinct—the eros. A fusion of the two instincts ensues, and gives rise to sadism. In order to escape being destroyed by its own death-instinct, the organism employs its narcissistic or self-regarding libido to force the former outward, and direct it against its objects. Freud considers this process as fundamental for the person's sadistic relations to his objects. I should say, moreover, that

---

[22] *Beyond the Pleasure Principle.* Eng. trans. 1942, p. 66.

parallel with this deflection of the death-instinct outward against objects, an intrapsychic reaction of defence goes on against that part of the instinct which could not be thus externalized. For the danger of being destroyed by this instinct of aggression sets up, I think, an excessive tension in the ego, which is felt by it as an anxiety, so that it is faced at the very beginning of its development with the task of mobilizing libido against its death-instinct. It can, however, only imperfectly fulfil this task, since, owing to the fusion of the two instincts, it can no longer, as we know, effect a separation between them. A division takes place in the id, or instinctual levels of the psyche, by which one part of the instinctual impulses is directed against the other."

"This apparently earliest measure of defence on the part of the ego constitutes, I think, the foundation-stone of the development of the super-ego, whose excessive violence in this early stage would thus be accounted for by the fact that it is an offshoot of very intense destructive instincts, and contains, along with a certain proportion of libidinal impulses, very large quantities of aggressive ones."

"This view of the matter makes it also less puzzling to understand why the child should form such monstrous and phantastic images of his parents. For he perceives his anxiety arising from his aggressive instincts as fear of an external object, both because he has made that object their outward goal, and because he has projected them on to it so that they seem to be initiated against himself from that quarter[23]."

We have now, I hope, sufficient material for a psycho-analytical interpretation of our fairy-tale. The Beast is the image of those sadistic and destructive instincts which accumulate in the child's ego in the course of its early development, particularly during the first four years, when, as Melanie Klein says, we come across a super-ego of the most incredible and phantastic character. "We get to look upon the child's fear of being

---

[23] Op. cit., pp. 268/69.

devoured, or cut up, or torn to pieces, or its terror of being surrounded and pursued by menacing figures, as a regular component of its mental life; and we know that the man-eating wolf, the fire-spewing dragon, and all the evil monsters out of myths and fairy-stories flourish and exert their unconscious influence in the phantasy of each individual child, and it feels itself persecuted and threatened by those evil shapes[24]." Madame Leprince de Beaumont had the ability to recover such an image from her childhood memories, and to exorcise it by a myth of transformation. But the figure of the Beast is an image of the mother (who, significantly, has no place in the fairy-tale) projected with all the psychic significance of the narrator's archetypal animus: the mother who had had the power to grant or withhold the gratification of her needs, the externalized symbol of the death instincts, terrifying to Eros until transformed by the magic of love. The story seems to assume that at some earlier stage the daughter had been deprived of the mother's breast and her libido had therefore turned towards the father.

Aesthetic pleasure has been defined (by Adrian Stokes[25]) as "the perception of a reconstructed whole ... one built upon the recognition of the object's previous loss or ruin (whether or not this ruin is also shown) in contrast with manic denial. Art, if only by implication, bears witness to the world of depression or chaos overcome." *Beauty and the Beast* is a perfect allegory of such reconstruction or restitution. Ugliness (the Beast) we have previously defined as that which is unshapely, but as Burke warned us, it is not the opposite to proportion or fitness: it is consistent with an idea of the sublime, of *terribilità*. John Rickman, who was the first to look at the nature of ugliness from a psycho-analytical point of view, suggested that just as human psychology made greater progress when it gave recognition to the factors of mental pain, anxiety

---

[24] Ibid., p. 268.

[25] *Form in Art: A Psychoanalytical Interpretation.* "J. of Aesthetics and Art Criticism", vol. XVIII, no. 2 (1959), p. 198.

and guilt, so it would "seem prudent to accord more significance than is commonly done in the literature to these disturbing but powerful forces in our aesthetic inclinations, and to see whether the underlying impulses of destructiveness, which give rise to these painful feelings, do not provide a substratum to Art as they do to everyday life. ... The artist provides more than a momentary consolation for our miseries; he goes behind the veil which screens the source of our dejection and brings back evidence for the triumph of the creative impulse over the forces of destruction; he can do this not by the denial of pain but by facing it with a determination to master it[26]." But there is more to it than therapy and reparation, which indeed Rickman indicated in the final words of his paper: "Our need for beauty springs from the gloom and the pain we experience from our destructive impulses to our good and loved objects; our wish is to find in art evidence of the triumph of life over death; we recognize the power of death when we say a thing is ugly."

Dr. Hanna Segal, developing this theory twelve years later[27], defined ugliness as that which "expresses the state of the internal world in depression. It includes tension, hatred and its results—the destruction of good and whole objects and their change into persecutory fragments." Depression is a technical term in Kleinian analysis, derived from the loss of the loved object, the breast: a very complex group of anxieties. Dr. Segal is much more realistic, and more faithful to the aesthetic experience, because she recognizes that Rickman's definition does not allow for the continued presence of ugliness in the work of art: it assumes that ugliness is the contrary to beauty and must be transformed before there can be a satisfying aesthetic experience. But altogether apart from the ugly works of art I have mentioned, the ugly is always

---

[26] *On the Nature of Ugliness and the Creative Impulse,* "Int. J. Psycho-analysis" XXI, Part 3, 1940.
[27] *A Psycho-analytical Approach to Aesthetics,* "Int. J. Psycho-analysis" XXXIII, Part 11.

nakedly present in tragedy, even in comedy; indeed, in Dr. Segal's words, "the idea that ugliness is an essential component of a complete experience seems to be true of the tragic, the comic, the realistic, in fact of all the commonly accepted categories of the aesthetic except one"— "classical" beauty. And even in this case "all our analytical experience as well as the knowledge derived from other forms of art suggest that the deep experience (embodied in the classical work of art) must have been what we call, clinically, a depression, and that the stimulus to create such a perfect whole must have lain in the drive to overcome an unusually strong depression."

All this is in agreement with an aesthetics of the work of art which stems from Lipps and Riegl and is most succinctly represented by Worringer's theory of abstraction and empathy. As long ago as 1908, that is to say, long before the diffusion of the psycho-analytical theories we have discussed, Worringer wrote of "the polar antithesis between two forms of aesthetic enjoyment"—of, on the one hand, "the ego as the clouding of the greatness of a work of art, as a curtailment of its capacity for bestowing happiness", and, on the other hand, "the most intimate union between ego and work of art, which receives all its life from the ego alone". Further: "This dualism of aesthetic experience ... is ... not a final one. These two poles are only gradations of a common need, which is revealed to us as the deepest and ultimate essence of all aesthetic experience—the need for self-alienation." Popular usage, as Worringer points out, speaks with striking accuracy of "losing oneself" in the contemplation of a work of art. In this sense we can attribute all aesthetic enjoyment to the impulse of self-alienation. The need for empathy and the need for abstraction are the two poles of human aesthetic experience, one representing the only possibility of repose, not only from the confusion and obscurity of the external world, but also from the confusion and obscurity of the internal world in depression; the other representing immersion in the immediate and the organic, the condition being that the work of art reflects natural organic tendencies in man and permits him, in Worringer's words, "in aesthetic perception, to flow uninhibitedly with his inner feeling of vitality, with his inner need for activity, into the felicitous current of this formal happening. So that, borne along by this inexpressible, inapprehensible movement, he experiences that absence of desire which makes its appearance the moment man—delivered from the differentiation of the individual consciousness—is able to enjoy the unclouded happiness of his purely organic being[28]."

This dualism corresponds to the facts of the history of art, and though the antitheses, in principle, are mutually exclusive (as we might demonstrate in the extremes of contemporary art, expressionism and constructivism), nevertheless in actual fact, as Worringer again points out, "the history of art represents an unceasing disputation between the two tendencies[29]". Personally I have always clung to the supposition, as Ruskin did, that there is a possibility of reconciliation, of synthesis: that all the many antitheses or oppositions we use to describe our psychological and aesthetic experiences—abstraction and empathy, style and naturalism, form and feeling, beautiful and ugly—all these in certain rare works of art find a perfect balance. Ruskin thought he had found that balance in what he called a piece of "mathematic sculpture", the tomb of Ilaria del Caretto in Lucca Cathedral carved in the year 1406 by Jacopo della Quercia; of which he wrote[30] that it is the only piece of monumental work known to him in the world "which unites in perfect and errorless balance the softest mysteries of emotion with the implacable severities of science". The mysteries of emotion revealed by psycho-analysis can hardly be described as "soft"; nor does science in aesthetic form remain

---

[28] *Abstraction and Empathy: a Contribution to the Psychology of Style.* Trans. by MICHAEL BULLOCK from the 11th German edition. London (Routledge & Kegan Paul) 1953.

[29] Ibid., p. 45.

[30] In: *The Schools of Art in Florence* (1874).

implacably severe; but that integration of the personality which is the aim of psycho-analysis, and that "reserve and restraint of power" represented in a work of art such as the tomb of Ilaria, is perfectly symbolised in the marriage of Beauty and the Beast.

"Beauty", said the fairy in our story, "come and receive the reward for the choice you have made; you have preferred virtue to beauty and wit, and now you deserve to find all these qualities in the one you love. You will become a great queen; may your throne not destroy your virtue."

There is an epilogue to the story. Integral to the fairy-tale are the two sisters of Beauty, whose hearts, as we have already noted, were full of envy. I cannot now enlarge on the significance of envy in psychoanalysis, but it is fundamental. It is the factor that destroys human happiness and it has its roots in the Oedipal situation. When in the story the father returned from the castle for the first time, he brought with him the rose that Beauty had asked for, and when he gave it to her, he said: "Here you are, Beauty, take this rose. It has cost your father very dear." The two sisters then turned on Beauty and heaped all the blame upon her. "See", they cried, "what this miserable little creature's pride has brought us to! Why couldn't she ask for sensible things as we did! But oh no, Miss Beauty must always be different. And now she has been the means of condemning our father to death, she doesn't even weep."

The rose is a symbol of what all the sisters desire, but which only Beauty has succeeded in obtaining. This is the basis of the intense envy of the elder sisters. When at the end of the story the fairy turns to them, she says: "I know your little hearts and all the malice they contain. You will become two statues, yet keep your reason within the stone that shall embalm you. You will stand forever at the gate of your sister's castle and I impose no other punishment on you than this: that you must watch and witness her happiness. You can break the spell the moment you recognize your own faults, but I'm very much afraid you will always remain as statues. For though one may correct pride, bad temper, greediness and sloth, only a miracle can take envy from the heart."

And that is the conclusion of the analysts about feminine envy in general. Only a miracle, a strong incentive combined with a capacity for self-sacrifice such as Beauty manifested, gives a woman, wrote Melanie Klein[31], in individual instances, the capacity for such a very exceptional achievement as the overcoming of what is known as the castration complex, the deep source of envy and sadism. This may explain, not only the prevalence of envy in the feminine heart, but also the comparative rarity of works of art created by women.

---

[31] Op. cit., p. 212.

A. Hilary Armstrong

The Divine Enhancement of
Earthly Beauties
The Hellenic and Platonic Tradition

This paper comes out of and is part of a lifetime's attempt to make present to our very different world the great Platonists of the first centuries of our era and the Hellenic tradition within which they imagined, thought and worshipped. This attempt has been increasingly inspired in more recent years by a sense of contemporary urgency. A very curious and distinctive feature of European culture is its double religious foundation in two different ways of thinking about the divine, the Hellenic and the Biblical. The full implications of this have not been realized till recently, when the manifest disintegration of our "inherited conglomerate", our complex and not altogether consistent spiritual and intellectual inheritance, has led both to the rapid advance of quite new kinds of materialism and rationalism and to the search for a new kind of spirituality, a new understanding and awareness of the divine. In this search the work of Jung and of Eranos has been of central importance. Many have tried to find this new understanding by a free interpretation of at least some of what is given in the developed Christian tradition with its strong Hellenic elements, or, if they identify the Hellenic inheritance too closely with its critical-rationalist side from which Enlightenment thought developed, by a reaction to what is considered a more primitive, "Biblical", sort of Christianity. But there has also been a strong tendency, apparent in the work of Eranos over the years, to look for it in the great spiritual traditions of the East, of which we have come to know so much more in this century, and in the archaic spiritualities of the Old and New Worlds. And in the last two or three decades the great increase in our knowledge and understanding of the thought and piety of late Graeco-Roman antiquity, and especially of those last Hellenic Platonists whom we call Neoplatonists, has brought some of us to understand that we have here a vital link with Oriental spiritualities and archaic piety which is firmly present and of great influence and importance in our own complex tradition. The question of the relationship of the philosophy of Plotinus to the thought of India has been discussed since the publication of E. Bréhier's *La Philosophie de Plotin* in 1928, and I have been aware of it all my working life. But when I began to make my own, admittedly rather touristic and superficial, excursions of mind and spirit into the worlds of Indian thought[1] and of esoteric Islam I came to understand more clearly than ever before the value of the treasures which we have inherited from the philosophy and piety of late antiquity, because I came to see how many of them we hold in common with the East. This is a matter of great importance in our urgent search for a spirituality which will meet our present needs and be rooted in our ancient depths, as a spirituality must be if it is to live and grow. It will help our quest and increase the meaning of what we find if we understand that, when we venture into the great realms of Eastern spiritual experience, though the differences from the world we know are many and profound, we are not walking on altogether alien soil. The flowers we enjoy and the fruits we try to gather sometimes grow on plants and trees of which there are species native to, and to be found flourishing in, the soils and climates of our own tradition.

My subject is the way in which, in the Hellenic tradition, the beauties of earth and the beauties of the gods, or the divine, or

---

1 Here I have been very greatly helped by my friend and colleague at Dalhousie University, Professor Ravi Ravindra. An example of our close collaboration in the study of our respective traditions is "*Buddhi* in the *Bhagávadgita* and *Psyche* in Plotinus" in Religious Studies 15 (September 1979) pp. 327-342: also published in *Neoplatonism and Indian Thought* ed. R. Baine Harris (Norfolk, Virginia 1982) pp. 63-86.

God, are apprehended together, so that earthly beauties stimulate and provide expression for awareness of divine presence, and, in turn, the sense of divine presence enhances earthly beauties. I shall begin by considering this in the old pre-philosophical and non-philosophical awareness of divine beauty in the beauties of earth which continued to surround and stimulate philosophical awareness of the divine down to the end of the ancient world. Then I shall go on to show how in the Platonic, and particularly the late Platonic, philosophical tradition the sense of divine enhancement of earthly beauty persists and develops in a most powerful and influential form.

The beauties with which we shall be concerned are primarily natural beauties, including of course in an eminent degree the beauties of human bodies. The beauties of works of art, though sometimes highly esteemed, occupy generally a rather modest place in Hellenic sensibility. One does not meet many aesthetes in the ancient world, and ancient "philosophies of art" have to be painstakingly constructed by moderns who have this sort of concern from, generally rather incidental, observations in contexts where the main interests of the philosophers do not lie in the appreciation of works of art. The kind of beauty with which philosophers are most concerned is of course not the beauty of nature or of artefacts but moral and spiritual beauty, the beauty of souls, not of bodies. This should always be borne in mind, but should not be misunderstood. In the Hellenic tradition the awareness of and appreciation of moral excellence and spiritual majesty, in humans or gods, is not cut off from or apprehended as something intrinsically different from awareness and appreciation of the beauties of earth. Moral beauties for the philosophers certainly rank higher in the scale of beauties than the beauties of bodies. But it is a continuous scale and the beauties are all really beauties. Moral and aesthetic philosophy are not separately distinguishable, still less separable, in the Hellenic tradition. In anachronistic modern terms one might say that Hellenic ethics are a sort of moral aesthetics. And in the Platonic tradition the quest for God is always driven on by the love which is the response to beauty, and only to beauty.

I

In considering what non-philosophical Greeks felt and thought about earthly beauty and its divine enhancement I shall be guided mainly by the poets. The ancient sacred sites, and the poor remnants which we have of the mass of works of visual art, sculptures and paintings, which adorned them, can tell us something, but not perhaps very much, about how the ancients responded to the beauties of earth: any general statements about this, based, as they would have to be, to a great extent on our own response to the sites in their present state and the works of art which we have, would be insecurely founded. But the poets can, if we read them carefully, help us to understand a good deal. At first reading it may seem that they do not tell us very much. They do not, as a rule, dilate on their own feelings or write pages of the sort of rich description which can sometimes be found in later European or in Eastern literatures. Hellenistic sensibility seems closer to other literary sensibilities here than classical. But in reading the greatest of Hellenistic poets and the one most successful at giving a vivid impression of the beauties of earth, Theocritus, one is struck by the economy of his vivid descriptions and the way in which they are firmly integrated into and support the story: one can perceive this very well, for instance, at the beginning of the *Thyrsis* (Idyll I) or the end of the *Thalysia* (Idyll VII) or the description of the spring in the *Hylas* (Idyll XIII 39-45). We may note particularly in this last that there is only one little phrase, though a marvellous one, about the beauty of the Nymphs who catch Hylas, *eär th' horoōsa Nycheia*, "Nycheia with her look of Spring". When Theocritus gives us some real lush gush about beauty it is about the artificial beauty of Queen Arsinoe's Adonis celebration, and it is put into the mouths of those silly chattering women Gorgo and Praxinoa and of the singer whose song suits their taste so admirably. (*Adoniazousae*, Idyll XV, 78-86 and 100-144.) I am not, of course, suggesting for a moment that Theocritus is intending to be rude or satirical about the show. A poet who desires royal patronage is not rude about religious entertainments put on by the Queen. At the most he is expecting his readers to be aware of a slight inflection of tone, or to observe him with their minds' eye raising his eyebrows slightly.

The character of the Greek poetic way of evoking earthly beauty can be particularly well appreciated when we turn to the sort of human or human-divine beauty which in other literatures gives occasion for rich and lavish description. We can see its quality very well in the most famous of evocations of the most famous beauty, the appearance of Helen on the walls of Troy (*Iliad* III 139-160). This was remembered and kept its power down through the centuries. Norman Baynes, following Psellos, recalls how it was remembered and used in eleventh-century Constantinople: "In the eleventh century when the beautiful Caucasian mistress of the Emperor first appeared by his side in a public procession to the hippodrome a courtier expressed his admiration in two words, *ou nemesis*, 'it were no shame...'. The lady saw the impression created by the quotation, but did not understand: she summoned the courtier to her side and asked for an explanation. But for the court of Byzantium those two words from Homer had sufficed to conjure up the picture of the old men on the walls of Troy who gazing at Helen in her radiance said, *ou nemesis*, 'It were no shame that men should fight for such as she'."[2] But when we read this most powerful of Greek celebrations of an earthly beauty we find that there is not a word of description in it of what that beauty looked like. Baynes' romantic "radiance" seems to come from the "shimmering garments" in which Helen wraps herself before setting out in line 141. And what the old men at the Skaian gates

2 Norman Baynes "The Hellenistic Civilisation and East Rome" (*Byzantine Studies* I, London, Athlone Press 1955) pp. 22-23, referring to Psellos, *Chronographia* VI 61.

said in their high chirping voices, and the Byzantine courtier
alluded to, was simply

> Surely there is no blame on Trojans and strong-greaved Achaeans
> if for long time they suffer hardship for a woman like this one.
> Terrible is the likeness of her face to immortal goddesses.
> Still, though she be such, let her go away in the ships, lest
> she be left behind, a grief to us and our children.[3]

And if we turn from this to ancient descriptions of the theophanies
of goddesses, in which they appear in their full beauty and glory,
we do not get much nearer to knowing what they looked like.
When Aphrodite manifests herself to Anchises after she has been
to bed with him,[4] all we read is that she grew so tall that her head
touched the roof and that the sort of beauty which Aphrodite has
shone from her face. It is a description of the event according to
the proper formula for theophanies, though not necessarily less
powerful for that. We can perhaps feel the power of this standard
description more in the two great theophanies of Demeter in the
Eleusis hymn.[5] In both she grows taller and a light shines round
her: in the second and more solemn, after she has commanded the
institution of her cult at Eleusis, the light grows more intense, like
lightning, and there is a fragrance about her: and, to show clearly
that she has returned from her appearance as an old woman to the
everlasting youth which belongs to the gods, we are told that her
hair flows golden over her shoulders. The Eleusis hymn contains
other good examples of this terse and powerful evocation of
beauty, the picture of the daughters of Celeus running down the
road to fetch the disguised goddess and the old lady in her long
dark robe following them back (174-183) and Persephone among
the flowers at the beginning (1-14). In this scene, which has
inspired so many imaginations down the centuries, Persephone's
beauty gets a couple of conventional epithets and of the great

---

3 *Iliad* III 156-160 tr. Richmond Lattimore.
4 Homeric Hymn V *To Aphrodite* 172-175.
5 Homeric Hymn II *To Demeter* 188-189 and 275-280.

narcissus which fatally attracts her we hear only about its size and that "the broad sky above and the whole earth and the salt wave of the sea laughed because of its fragrance" (14).

In all these passages what is evoked is a whole scene and its impact upon the participants. It is the power rather than the aesthetic enjoyability of beauty which is brought out: and this is particularly so where there is anything explicitly divine or godlike about the beauties evoked, as there generally is where they are experienced with some intensity. We can see very well how this works in the most powerful of all ancient evocations of the non-human beauties of earth, in the *Oedipus at Colonus* of Sophocles. When Antigone describes to her blind father the beauty of the sacred wood of Colonus, with its strong growth of laurel, olive and vine and its crowd of nightingales (16-18) and when the old men of the village elaborate her description in the first part of the most memorable of Sophoclean choruses (668-692), what is evoked is well summed up in the first words of Antigone's description *chōros d'hod' hiros*, "this place is holy" (16). When the beauties of earth are experienced intensely they are experienced as beauties with something divine in them. And of course the divine to the ancients, though always beautiful, is not just beautiful in a way to which the proper response is a comfortable sort of aesthetic enjoyment. Those who know the passages which I have just referred to in their contexts will understand very well that where there is divine manifestation there is at least a potency of terror. I shall return to this later.

We now need to consider something about this older awareness of the divine in the beauties of earth which will become important when we begin to think about the relationship to it of the Platonic understanding of the way in which the divine is present in them. This is that it is awareness of the divine in one single world, the only one there is, but awareness of it, not in a bland uniformity of presence but in an innumerable diversity. In the old way of thinking, feeling and imagining which is that of the Greeks and other Mediterranean peoples, as of all archaic cultures, there is only one world and it is divine. There is no question of the divine belonging to and intervening from a higher or different sphere or world. The gods are born in the world. They do not make it. The history of the generation of the world is the family history of the gods. The starting-point for awareness of divine enhancement of the world's beauties is a general awareness of divinity present everywhere and an apprehension of it as part of all experience. How, then, can we speak of a divine *enhancement* of earthly beauty when all earthly beauty is divine? We can, in a very real sense, because in the Greek, as in all archaic cultures, there is an intense awareness of the *poikilia* of the one divine world, of the continual variations in kind and degree of the divine manifestations in its beauty. So the awareness of the divine in the world is not vague or undifferentiated. It is apprehended specially, in varying ways and degrees of intensity, in innumerable theophanies, special moments, special signs, precise disclosure-places. It is these which continually enhance and intensify the sense of the divine beauty: all sorts of particular natural signs, from thunder on the mountains to a sudden flight of birds: a visit to a great holy place or, more often, to a little one, a local spring or a shrine at the end of one's own fields: the apprehension of the beauty of a particular person imaginatively intensified by memories of the manifestations of divine beauties in earlier poetry, of the sort which I spoke about in the preceding paragraphs. That light-hearted but also intensely devout poem of Sappho which begins *Poikilothron' athanat' Aphrodita* gives, I believe, an appropriate instance of this kind of little theophany in its opening verses:

> Aphrodite, undying in intricate splendour,
> Child of the Father, braider of snares, I beg you
> Do not, Our Lady, with torments and tribulations
> Crush me in spirit,
> But come! Come here, if ever in time beforehand
> Hearing my cries afar you attended, and leaving
> The golden house of your Father you came to me, yoking
> Birds to your chariot.
> Then the quick beautiful sparrows brought you, circling,

Wings beating thick and fast, over the dark earth,
Down from the sky through the bright air, and suddenly
There they were with me.[6]

"There *they* were with me." It seems that what touched off
Sappho's awareness of the presence of her goddess was a sudden
flight of small birds into a bush or tree near her, which can be a
numinous occurrence to those attuned to this sort of thing.

The divine powers who were experienced as present in and as
intensifying the beauties of earth included many who were
apprehended as especially wild, dark, and terrifying (there is
always some degree of terror in the manifestations of the divine).
The mountain, the high wild lands always very close to the farms
and cities, had its own powers. There was Artemis, in her very
ancient aspect as Lady of the wild beasts. There was Pan, a genial
enough character in most of his manifestations, but master of his
own special terror. And the many-sided Dionysus was master of
the most terrible of mountain powers, the madness which drove
out the women to the mountain – running and dancing of which
the climax was the tearing of living flesh. The Greeks very well
knew that divine beauty could send men mad. Aphrodite and Erōs
had their own kind of maddening power, more universal than the
mountain-madness of Dionysus, that prehistoric but vividly
remembered and ritually re-enacted experience whose beauty and
terror are so well conveyed to us by Euripides in the *Bacchae*. It is
important to remember that the wild beauty of the mountain
powers was never cut off from or opposed to the tamer world of
farm and city. Artemis, sometimes, notably at Ephesus, in a very
different but equally ancient and authentic aspect, could be a great
city goddess. Pan demanded, and got, a cave-shrine under the
Acropolis in the very middle of Athens, and seems to have been
perfectly settled and happy there.[7] Dionysus lived on the best of
terms with Apollo at Delphi, where the most powerful ritual re-
enactment of the mountain running took place, and presided over

6 Sappho I (191 D. L. Page *Lyrica Graeca Selecta*) tr. A. H. A.
7 Herodotus VI 105-106.

the most sophisticated of city entertainments in his theatres and the jolliest and most bawdy phallic revels on the farms.

Not only the terrifying powers of the wild but the powers of darkness are included in the world-enhancing and beauty-enhancing divine presence of which the Greeks were aware. The powers of darkness, the powers in the earth, were not of course for the Greeks powers of evil. I need not at an Eranos meeting stress the importance of this Hellenic awareness of divinity on the dark side of things. We are probably all aware of the disadvantages of a world-view which understands the cosmos and the things which happen in it in terms of a battle between the good forces of light and the evil forces of darkness. I shall speak briefly later about what happens to this sense of the divinity of the dark in the Platonic tradition. One of the best ways of coming to understand what it meant in the older Hellenic world with which we are at present concerned is a prolonged meditation on the *Eumenides* of Aeschylus and the *Oedipus at Colonus* of Sophocles. In both plays we are concerned with the most terrible of the dark powers in the earth, the Eumenides who are also the Erinyes. In Aeschylus our understanding of them progresses from the, perhaps somewhat melodramatic, horror of the beginning to the splendour of the end when they are conducted in the great procession to the shrine which everyone in the audience knew, neither defeated nor transformed but persuaded by Athenē to show to her people that other aspect of which all their worshippers were aware. And, going on to Colonus, we find that the beloved and beautiful sacred wood of which I spoke earlier is pre-eminently the wood of the Eumenides. We find that, for all the terror they inspire in the villagers, the ritual for their propitiation which is described with loving care by the Chorus has an austere beauty appropriate to ancient powers of good and is no grotesque apotropaic ceremony for averting the machinations of demons (466-492). And, from the prayer of Oedipus (84-110) to the closing scene, we see them working together with Apollo (to whom they are never reconciled in Aeschylus' play) for that final consummation, in some way good for Oedipus and for Athens, whose nature is best left to Sophocles to suggest.

Wild and tame, mad and sane, dark and light: in all these the divine is present, and where it is present there is an intensified beauty.

II

Before going on from the presence of the divine in the earthly beauties of the one world of the old Hellenic tradition to the Platonic awareness of the beauty-enhancing presence of a divine which is in some sense separate and transcendent, it will be desirable to say something about a way of thinking, feeling and imagining which has had a very powerful effect on the later thoughts and imaginations of Europeans. This is cosmic piety or religiosity. It is highly relevant to our theme that we should consider this and its consequences, and should distinguish it both from the older Greek experience of divinity in the beauties of the world and from what I believe to be authentic Platonism, more precisely than the ancients themselves always did and some moderns have done. Cosmic piety, like so much else in later ancient thought, does have its effective beginnings in Plato: and the early Stoics, with their passionate sense of the total unity of divine and world, developed it strongly. But the form in which it became lastingly powerful, which I propose to consider here, is that which it took as a result of a certain re-Platonizing and re-Aristotelianizing of Stoicism at some time not very long before the beginning of our era. This is the form which had such an immensely powerful influence on European thinking and imagining at least till the seventeenth century and still, I think, persists sometimes in many of our imaginations about the world and our selves. Its particular relevance at this point in this paper is that it carries in it a distinctive kind of pseudo-otherworldliness. There is for those who think and feel in this way only one world, the great divine material cosmos: though another spiritual and immaterial cosmos can be added outside and above the material one without any great disturbance of the structure of thought and feeling as long as it is thought of and imagined as outside and above. But the one cosmos is, as we shall see, very sharply and significantly divided into two, and the two parts are very differently valued.

The general picture of the world as it was seen by those who shared in the cosmic piety is familiar to anyone interested in the thought and imagination of late antiquity, the Middle Ages and the early Renaissance. But we should consider it rather carefully if we are to understand its consequences as they concern us here. Those who apprehended the world in this way still saw it as a great divine living organism, and thought of their own true rational selves as parts of the divine fire which animated and governed it. But that divine fire, whose animating and ordering presence on and around our earth was not of course denied, was thought of as predominantly concentrated in the Upper Cosmos, the region of the heavenly bodies, the intensely living and supremely intelligent visible gods, and it was there that men had to look if they were to see divinity in its true beauty and glory. These heavenly bodies were believed to be of vast size and to circle the earth in vast orbits, in accordance with the scientific astronomy of the Platonic and Aristotelian schools: we should never, of course, forget that a most important reason for the perdurance of the cosmic piety through so many centuries and its hold on men's intellects and imaginations was that it was in accord with the best available physical science. The earth lies in the centre of this vast celestial universe, a mere point in size compared with the great fiery bodies of the heavens, surrounded by its dark, damp, mistily impure lower atmosphere. Beyond this, and beginning with the sphere of the moon, the regions of intense and splendid fiery light, where the living and divine globes of moon and sun and stars circle in their everlasting dance, stretch out to the outermost sphere of heaven, the sphere of the fixed stars. We should appreciate the importance to this system of the stroke of intellectual and imaginative genius which disposed of the "fixed stars", in their potentially embarrassing number and variety, by setting them all in a single sphere. Was, perhaps, one of the most shatteringly revolutionary consequences of the new astronomy the dissolution of the *Primum Mobile*?

Let us now consider the consequences of this view of the cosmos in so far as they are relevant to our subject. Quite a good way of beginning will be to try to relate it to the three co-equal titles of our conference. There is certainly in it an intense devout concentration on the "Beauty of the World", if "World" is taken to mean the cosmos as a whole and the concentration is understood to be on those greatest parts of it which predominantly make the ordered beauty of that whole. There is a full appreciation of "Die Schönheit der Dinge" if "Dinge" is understood selectively. The heavenly bodies are undoubtedly Things quite overwhelming in their thingness. But when we turn to our French title "La Beauté sur la Terre" we find that cosmic piety was liable to lead to a radical devaluation of and disesteem for the beauty on earth, if by earth we understand this little globe which is our home here and now. It is, I hope, by now generally understood that though the ancient picture of the cosmos was in the astronomical sense geocentric, the piety which accompanied it was by no means geocentric in its scale of values. The central earth is not only insignificantly small in comparison with the least of the heavenly bodies. This central region below the moon in which it lies is low in every way and on every scale, and the earth is lowest in it. It is the darkest, dampest and dirtiest part of the universe, a kind of cosmic cesspit, full of corruption and decay. Divinity and beauty are not of course entirely absent from it: it is still part of the divine universe. But its beauties are dimmed and spoilt and its delights transitory and corrupting. We should lift up our hearts and minds from them to see true divine beauty in the glory of the great fiery spheres of heaven and their everlasting dance. (You will notice that I speak of the heavenly bodies as "fiery", and this is what the Stoics and Platonists believed they were. Aristotle's doctrine of the

Quintessence, the fifth celestial element different from the four
here below, was not generally accepted by the devotees of the
divine cosmos. But this made very little difference in practice,
because they considered the heavenly fire to be so much purer and
more authentic than fire here below that the difference in degree
became almost a difference in kind.)

   We can begin to see already what I meant by speaking of the
"pseudo-otherworldliness" of cosmic piety. We shall see this even
more clearly if we turn from its way of thinking about the
macrocosm to its way of thinking about the microcosm. In my
general account of cosmic piety I remarked that its adherents
thought of their own true rational selves as being part of the divine
fire of the heavens. This meant that the true life of those souls was
thought of as being above in those visible heavens and that the
spiritual journey was thought of in terms of an ascent to that true
heavenly life, and the preparation for it by purging the soul of all
the impurities of earth. Here below the soul was clogged and
contaminated by the passions which belong to the dark impurities
of this lowest region. We encounter here in a very strong form the
ancient Greek opposition between the hot, bright, dry, active,
male, good divine principle and the cold, dark, moist, passive,
female, evil principle. (The characterization of the two principles
as male and female should always be remembered. It has very deep
roots and often produces very strange results in spiritualities
affected by this way of thinking.) When we take into account this
way of thinking and feeling about the soul and the spiritual life
we can see very clearly how radically "other-worldly" cosmic
piety is in the sense that it utterly despises and rejects the beauties
and delights of earth. I am inclined to think that both in later
antiquity and in the succeeding Christian centuries the rejection
of earth and its beauties becomes particularly sharp, violent and
harsh (and in Christians particularly anti-feminine) when this
corporealist spirituality of the cosmic piety is somehow consciously or unconsciously at work: and it penetrated so deep into
the religious outlook on the world that it can sometimes continue

to work in feelings and imaginations, when the world-picture to which it properly belongs has been consciously rejected or abandoned.

There is another way in which it is possible that cosmic piety may have affected the sensibility to beauty of those influenced by it and led to a despising of the common beauties of earth. From the time when the scientific astronomy of the Academy became dominant the Upper Cosmos was thought of as pre-eminently the realm in which mathematical reason and order were dominant. (Pre-Socratic views of *ta meteora*, "the things up above" were often very different.) In the cosmic piety the noble purity of the spherical form of the visible gods and the grand regularity of their circular movements were powerful incentives to devotion. We should notice again the religious importance of the basic simplicity of this great vision of the world. The ancient scientific astronomers might well have been able to cope with a more complex picture of the heavens, at least a little closer to our own understanding of the vast intricacy and strangeness of what goes on up there. But this would have been destructive of cosmic piety. It was essential to it that the glorious manifestation of divine reason in the heavens should be apprehensible and expressible in simple terms – the sphere, the perfect shape, and the circle of the choral dance, the perfect movement. Never have the rotund and the rotary been so religiously exalted. This devotion to simple and regular form and order may well have at least helped to intensify a tendency to despise the beauties of this earth with their endless variety of irregular shapes and unco-ordinated movements. Cosmic piety would tend to reinforce the "classicist" side of Hellenic sensibility, the preference for a beauty in which mathematical structure, symmetry and order can clearly be discerned, which was perhaps always in tension with that primaeval awareness of the *poikilia* of divine manifestation in the beauties of earth with which I began. I shall return to this subject when I come to speak of the thought of Plotinus.

III

The transition from the way in which the divine enhancement of earthly beauty was apprehended in the old Hellenic world to the way in which it was apprehended by the Platonists is generally presented as a transition from thinking of it in terms of one world to thinking of it in terms of two *cosmoi*, a material one and a spiritual or intelligible one: this is the true Platonic distinction, which needs to be carefully distinguished from that spatial distinction between Upper and Lower Cosmos which belongs to the cosmic piety we have just been considering, though the two often intermingle and even become somewhat confused in the thought of the ancients. The result of this Platonic way of thinking is that the divine enhancement of beauties by manifestation or theophany is interpreted in an "other-worldly" way as the appearance of a light and life from "beyond", from the incorporeal world only apprehensible by the intellect. There is of course a great deal of truth in this presentation. But if we simply leave it at that we shall be in danger of over-simplifying the Platonic understanding of the world and making too sharp a break between it and the old Hellenic awareness of divinity by which, to the end of antiquity, the Platonists were surrounded and in which they shared. This very simple fact that the context of Platonism was the old Hellenic piety needs to be continually remembered. The Platonists lived among the shrines and images of that older world: they practised its rites as a matter of course as members of Hellenic communities, and the greatest part of their education as children consisted in learning the poetry with which this paper began. This last observation was of course intended to recall Plato's own well-known hostility to that poetry. I do not propose in this paper to spend much time on the theme of the attitude of Plato and later Platonists to the arts. As I said at the beginning I am trying to concentrate our attention where the poets and philosophers concentrated theirs, on the beauty of nature and spirit. But something must be said at this point if the whole Platonic attitude to the beauties of earth is not to be misunderstood.[8] First of all, of course, we need to remember that by the time the Platonist understanding of theophany in the beauties of earth took its most powerful and influential form in the third century A.D. the old hostility to the poets and their piety had disappeared. Platonic and poetic religion had come together, and in the end it was the Neoplatonic philosophers of Athens who were the last defenders of the old Hellenic ways of recognizing and worshipping the Divine. They were well content that the Platonic imagination should be the old Hellenic imagination, as in fact it had never ceased to be.

On this point we should not over-simplify the attitude of Plato himself. In his treatments of the subject in the *Republic* and the *Laws* he is writing very much from the point of view of a Minister of Education who is also Prefect of the Congregation of Rites: he is considering, that is, what needs to be done about poetry in the interests of intelligent reform of education and public worship. (It is important in considering ancient thought about art to remember that, always in classical Greece and to a considerable extent still in Hellenistic and Roman times, it is considered as a public activity with which the public authorities must be concerned because it affects the well-being of the whole community.) Plato's lowly view of the ontological status of the work of art as the "representation of a semblance" (*phantasmatos mimēsis Republic* 598B) and his double-edged appreciations of poetic inspiration in the *Ion* and the *Phaedrus* fit in very well with his stance as reformer of faith and morals. But of course this position requires him to recognize fully the power of art and its consequent importance to the

8 In addition to the many well-known works on this well-worn subject (among which I have found Iris Murdoch's *The Fire and The Sun* [Oxford 1977] particularly helpful) I would like to draw attention to the thesis of my former pupil Astrid Brunner *The Metaphysical Relevance of Art: a study of contemporary aesthetic philosophy against the background of Platonic/Neo-Platonic metaphysics* (M.A. Thesis, Department of Classics, Dalhousie University, Halifax, Nova Scotia, Canada, Fall 1977). I have learnt a great deal from this and from our discussions in the course of its preparation.

community. He, like all other Greek philosophers, was well aware that true philosophers are very rare indeed – if they ever occur at all. He knew that the great mass of mankind would always, even in the most ideal society which he could conceive, have to find such awareness of divinity as they were capable of through their feelings and imaginations, in their apprehensions of the beauties of this material world stimulated by the right sort of art. And he knew that this was how even those who might later become true philosophers would have to start: they could not even begin the philosophic quest which might lead, after many years, to the vision of the Forms and of the Good, unless their feelings and imaginations were rightly trained by a right awareness of divine beauty in this world. This is splendidly expressed in the great passage on the proper function of poetry, music and the visual arts in the education of the future philosopher-rulers in the Republic (III 401B-402A). And when we look at Plato's ideal proposals for the ordering of religion (he was very well aware that the political and social orders which he proposed as ideals, or as the best theoretically possible, were unrealisable, or very unlikely to be realised, in practice) we find that, though liturgical texts are to be drastically censored and reformed, all the old divine rites and ceremonies and holy places which enhanced the beauty of earth for ordinary men are assumed as still there, part of the continuing background for ordinary men and philosophers alike.[9] Plato's apprehension of the divine in this world at the level of feeling and imagination was not after all so far from the old Hellenic way. He was more critical, as was appropriate to his time and place, of inherited religious traditions than his very traditionalist successors. But he might not have been so hostile to their rather wholesale and uncritical defence of all the old natural pieties of the Mediterranean world against alien barbarian attack as Christian

9 This is clearly implied in the statement that the religious ordering of the ideal *Politeia* is to be left to the Delphic Oracle (*Republic* IV 427B). *Laws* V 738B-E is a very strong affirmation of the necessity for the city to preserve all traditional shrines and observances.

apologists would have liked him to be. There is no suggestion anywhere in his writings that he wanted or would have approved a "new religion" in the sense in which Christianity was a "new religion".

In considering how the Platonists understand the divine enhancement of earthly beauties we need to think carefully about the way in which their two *cosmoi* are related. I shall say more about this when I come to discuss the thought of Plotinus, but some preliminary remarks are necessary here to avoid misunderstanding. One of the few uncontroversial (I hope) remarks which can be made about the Platonic Forms is that they are incorporeal and perceptible only by the intellect. It was Plotinus who most fully worked out the implications of this. But I think it would be true to say that already in Plato it means that the Forms should not be thought of as "separate" in the sense of being outside, beyond, or above the material world. What their separation means is that they are independent of the particular instantiations of them perceived by the senses and prior to them both in being and thought. The material world owes such existence as it has to the Forms; they do not owe their existence to it and could perfectly well exist without it. And we can only understand our sense-perceptible cosmos in terms of the Forms, not the other way round. But there is no spatial separation, because they are not in space at all. (They are not in time either, but some very difficult and controversial questions arise here about the meaning of eternity in Plato and the Platonists and the relation of eternity to time which it would not be relevant to pursue here.[10]) However, Plato did sometimes see them imaginatively and portray them mythically as "outside" and "above". He did this with special power in the enormously influential mythical part of the *Phaedrus*, where the Forms are

10 Some idea of the problems which arise here can be gained from J. Whittaker, *God Time Being* (*Symbolae Osloenses Fasc. Supplet* XXIII, Oslo 1971): A. H. Armstrong "Eternity, Life and Movement in Plotinus' accounts of *Nous*" (*Plotinian and Christian Studies*, London 1979, XV) and P. Manchester "Time and the Soul in Plotinus, III 7 [45] 11" in *Dionysius* II (1978) pp. 102-136.

situated outside the heaven in the *huperouranios topos* (247C-E). This is very natural: the symbolism of light from above is very ancient and powerful. Do even those who have the most spiritual conception of God and the most intimate awareness of his presence here below always manage to avoid envisaging him as enthroned "above the sky"? But we must make the effort required to break away from this if we are to understand Platonic transcendence rightly.

This tendency to envisage the Forms as "up there" in spatial separation was reinforced, perhaps for Plato himself in his later years, and certainly for later Platonists, by that sharp emphasis on the spatially separate and transcendent divinity of the Upper Cosmos which was characteristic of the cosmic piety discussed earlier (pp. 59-63). And the tendency to make a very sharp separation between the intelligible and material worlds would also be reinforced by a literal interpretation of the *Timaeus* which set paradigm and copy apart with the Craftsman between them, and, later, by the Judaeo-Christian preference for a demiurgic or "artisan" understanding of creation.

An understanding of Platonic *erōs*, the passionate (in a modern, not the ancient sense[11]) drive towards beauty, is of course essential for any appreciation of Platonic thought about earthly beauties

---

11 It is most important in considering ancient thought about "the passions"' to remember how vividly aware the ancients remained that *pathos* and *passio* denote passivity. There is something feeble and soft about being dominated and marked by one's passions. The passionate person is not only pathĕtic but pathĕtic from the point of view of the ancient philosophers. Admittedly this is rather difficult to square with the Platonic doctrine of *erōs* which we are considering. William Blake brings out the difference between the ancient and the modern understanding of "passion" in a passage which, like so much in his writings, is consciously anti-Platonic in intention but deeply Platonic in feeling: "Men are admitted into Heaven not because they have curbed and governed their Passions or have no Passions but because they have cultivated their Understandings. The Treasures of Heaven are not Negations of Passion but Realities of Intellect, from which all the Passions Emanate Uncurbed in Their Eternal Glory. The Fool shall not enter into Heaven let him be never so Holy." (*Description of the Vision of the Last Judgement* p. 87 of *Additions to Blake's*

and their divine enhancement. Beauty for Platonists is what is lovable in a strong and vehement sense. And it seems that the *erōs* which drives the philosopher on to the vision of intelligible beauty is not different in kind from the commonest erotic *erōs*. This means that beauty at any level is always beauty because it always arouses *erōs*. The passage in the *Dialogues* on the ascent to the vision of absolute beauty which has most powerfully inspired later Platonists is of course Diotima's account of the final mysteries of *Erōs* in the *Symposium* (210A-212B). And if we read it carefully we shall find that it can tell us a good deal about the presence of absolute divine beauty in the beauties of earth.[12] The question which concerns us here is whether Plato intends to represent Diotima in her account of the ascent as recommending the kicking away of the steps at each stage, so that one is left at the end with a purely abstract contemplation of ultimate beauty which has no connexion with the particular beauties here below, and cannot enhance our awareness of them by a sense of its divine presence in them. I do not think that this is Plato's intention. To begin with, one has to start the ascent with a particular earthly beauty (210A, 4-8). This is in perfect accord with the *Phaedrus*, and I think that always in Plato a strong awareness of and a strong response to particular earthly beauties is the starting-point for the philosophical ascent. Plotinus expounds Plato's teaching excellently here in the first two chapters of his treatise *On Dialectic* (I 3 [20]). Then, at every stage from beginning to end, the universal and absolute beauty is present *in* particular beauties and is apprehended as what makes them beautiful (210 A8-B6 : 211 B2). Further, at each stage

Catalogue of Pictures etc. for 1810: p. 842 in *Poetry and Prose of William Blake* ed. Geoffrey Keynes, Nonesuch Press, 1927).

12 My exegesis of the *Symposium* is my own. But I have been greatly helped in it by the work which my former pupil, Elena Corrigan and I did on the dialogue in the course of the preparation of her thesis *The Structure of the Symposium* (M. A. Thesis, Department of Classics, Dalhousie University, Halifax, Nova Scotia, Fall 1979) which is a notable contribution to the understanding of the dialogue.

it is quite as important to expand horizontally as to ascend
vertically: the move from particular to universal is at least as
necessary as the move from lower to higher. To cling to one
particular *epitēdeuma* is as petty and slavish as to cling to a
particular human being (210D 1-2), and when one arrives at the
vision it is as clear that absolute beauty is not a *logos* or an *epistēmē*
as that it does not have hands or face (211A 5-7). I think that at the
end all the steps are still there, and once one has the abiding vision
of absolute beauty in one, one can go up and down them as one
needs, and will then see lower beauties, even bodily and earthly
ones, as enhanced by the divine presence in them of Beauty Itself.

There is another consideration about Platonic other-worldliness
which needs to be borne in mind when we are assessing how far it
is congruous with a strong sense of the divine enhancement of
earthly beauties. What is the precise nature of the love and
enjoyment of things here below which Plato and the Platonists
urge their followers to overcome and escape from? This is
something so commonplace to them, as to all great traditional
moralists, Eastern and Western, that it is not always very much
stressed, and this can lead to a misunderstanding of their true
position. It is not stressed in the *Symposium*, but it is certainly
there. In the passage which we are considering, the rather
unexpected appearance of "gold and fine clothes" along with
pretty boys among the things which Diotima says that one who
has experienced the vision will no longer care about (211D 2-3),
shows that the sort of attachment to earthly beauties which Plato,
here as elsewhere, is most concerned to draw people away from, is
the acquisitive and exploitative kind, with its endless fuss and
worry about *possessing* and *using* the good things of this world.
This is strongly confirmed by the portrayal of Socrates by
Alcibiades as the best of all exemplars in the matter of *erōs* because
he is so utterly unattached and unacquisitive (216D-219E). What
the Platonic tradition, and with varying degrees of emphasis the
other great Greek philosophical traditions and the older and more
authentic Christian traditions, wish their followers to get rid of is

the acquisitiveness which not only makes it impossible to start the ascent to the divine but breeds envy, hatred, and strife among mankind. They wish to eliminate desire for what Aristotle, following a lead given by Plato (*Phaedo* 66C 5-7), calls in a fine chapter of the *Nicomachean Ethics* (IX 8) the *perimachēta agatha* "the goods people fight about" (1168b 19 and 1169a 21). In Plato, Aristotle, and the older moral traditions generally the truly desirable goods of this world on which most emphasis is laid are those which belong to the possession and practice of moral virtue. Our best Western traditions are very close here to the commendation of non-attached action in the *Bhagávad Gitā* (III-V). The non-attached enjoyment of earthly beauties is always considered spiritually important, especially by those Christians influenced by the later Platonic tradition, but for its fullest and most splendid celebration we have to look, not to antiquity but to seventeenth-century England.

It is to be found in the *Centuries of Meditations* of my country neighbour Thomas Traherne, son of a shoemaker in the city of Hereford and for some years parish priest of the not otherwise very notable village of Credenhill. The *Meditations* were written for friends, and Traherne left his manuscript unsigned and made no attempt to publish it in his short lifetime.[13] They were only identified as his and published in the early years of this century. A few quotations will give an idea of the force of his celebration of the beauties of earth, his exhortation to see God in them, and his preaching of non-attachment.

> ... your Enjoyment of the World is never right, till you so Esteem it, that evry thing in it, is more your Treasure, then a Kings Exchequer full of Gold and Silver. And that Exchequer yours also in its Place and Service. Can you take too much joy in your fathers Works? He is Himself in evry Thing. Som Things are little on

13 Traherne lived from 1637 to 1674. Details of his life and works and of the rediscovery of the poems and *Meditations* are to be found in *Centuries, Poems and Thanksgivings* ed. H. M. Margoliouth, 2 vols (Oxford Clarendon Press 1958) and the more generally accessible *Poems, Centuries and Three Thanksgivings* ed. Anne Ridler, (London, Oxford University Press, 1966).

the outside, and Rough and Common: but I remember the Time, when the Dust of the Streets were as precious as Gold to my infant Eys, and now they are more precious to the Ey of Reason. (I. 25).

Wine by its moisture quencheth my Thirst, whether I consider it or no: but to see it flowing from his Lov who gav it unto Man, Quencheth the Thirst even of the Holy Angels. To consider it is to drink it Spritualy. To Rejoice in its Diffusion is to be of a Publick Mind. And to take Pleasure in all the Benefits it doth to all is Heavenly, for so they do in Heaven. (I. 27).

You never Enjoy the World aright till the Sea itself floweth in your Veins, till you are Clothed with the Heavens, and Crowned with the Stars. (I. 29).

When I came into the Country, and being seated among silent Trees, had all my Time in my own Hands, I resolved to Spend it all, whatever it cost me, in Search of Happiness, and to Satiat that burning Thirst which Nature had Enkindled in me from my Youth. In which I was so resolut, that I chose rather to liv upon 10 pounds a year, and to go in Lether Clothes, and feed upon Bread and Water, so that I might hav all my time clearly to my self: then to keep many Thousands per Annums in an Estate of Life where my Time would be Devoured in Care and Labor. (III 46).

He thought also that no Poverty could befall him that enjoyd Paradice: for when all the Things are gone which Men can giv, A Man is still as Rich as Adam was in Eden: who was Naked there. A Naked Man is the Richest Creature in all Worlds: and can never be Happy, till he sees the Riches of his Nakedness. He is very Poor in Knowledge that thinks Adam poor in Eden. (IV 36).

Traherne shows particularly clearly that the ideal pursued, often very unsuccessfully, by Platonists and Christians who share his love of this world is to enjoy to the full the beauties of earth and to be intensely aware of the divine presence in them, while eliminating as far as possible all desire to possess them and exploit them for transitory and illusory satisfactions.

It was above all Plotinus, in the third century of our era, who gave Platonism the form in which it has helped most to make us vividly aware of the divine presence in the beauties of earth. There are several reasons for this in his presentation of what he believed to be the true teaching of Plato. We are not in considering any of them concerned with ideas which Plotinus simply originated. A long development of thought in the Platonic and other Greek philosophical traditions lies behind them. But it was his presentation of them which gave them the power which they have exercised in the following centuries. The first and most important is Plotinus' insistence that the first principle and source of beauty and all goodness, the One or Good, completely transcends the Divine Intellect which is the World of Forms. Not only do Forms and Intellect originate from that which is neither form nor intellect. They are only beautiful in the true Platonic sense, that is delightful and lovable, capable of arousing *erōs*, because of the light and life from the Good which eternally plays upon them (VI 7 [38] 21-22).[14] Formal perfection, in the full sense of the finite perfection of the World of Forms which contains all real being, is not enough. It needs, and of course eternally receives, a light and life from the Formless which alone is what the soul driven on by the *erōs* which is given by that Good truly seeks. And if we look at Plotinus' divine world the other way up, from the point of view of what lies below Intellect, we discover something else relevant to our present subject. This is that there is another way in which the self-enclosed, inturned perfection of the Intellect which is the Forms is not enough for Plotinus. Pierre Hadot brings this out very well in his exposition of Plotinus' interpretation of Plato's least favourite myth, the story in Hesiod about Ouranos, Kronos and Zeus, in his great anti-gnostic work.[15] What is of particular interest to us here is Hadot's comment on the remarkable text in which Plotinus says:

> The king there in the higher world does not rule over different, alien people, but has the most just, the natural sovereignty and the true kingdom: for he is king of truth and natural lord of all his own offspring and divine company, king of the king and of the kings, and more rightly than Zeus called the father of the gods; Zeus imitates him in this way also in that he is not satisfied with the

14 VI 7 [38] 21-22. See A. H. Armstrong "Beauty and the Discovery of Divinity in The Thought of Plotinus", *Plotinian and Christian Studies* XIX.
15 The great work is Cilento's *Paideia Antignostica* and the German *Großschrift*, the work which Porphyry split into four treatises placed in different Enneads III 8, V 8, V 5 and II 9. See P. Hadot "Ouranos, Kronos and Zeus In Plotinus' Treatise Against the Gnostics" in *Neoplatonism and Early Christian Thought*, London 1981 pp. 124-137.

contemplation of his father but aspires to, we might say, the active power with which his grandfather established reality in being (V 5 [32], 16-24; tr. A. H. Armstrong).

The king here is of course the One or Good; the father of Zeus is the Divine Intellect which is the World of Forms; and Zeus, the grandson of the Good, is Soul. Hadot comments:

> There is a deep-seated affinity, so it appears, between the sovereignty of Zeus and the sovereignty of Ouranos, even though the sovereignty of Ouranos is wholly transcendent. Thus we discover in Plotinus' theory a hidden preference for the process of procession: the power characteristic of the One and of the Soul. ... the Beautiful is Beautiful above all for its own sake, for the sake of its conversion to itself; whereas the Good has no need to be Good for itself, because it has no need at all. The Good is Good only for things other than itself, in the movement of procession which it necessarily gives rise to. At root, it is this generosity of the Good which to Plotinus' way of thinking is the supreme value. Hence the principle, *bonum diffusivum sui*, the principle which, for Plotinus, explains and justifies the unfolding of the whole of reality.[16]

This primacy of generosity, of outgoing creativity, with its accompanying sense that absolute perfection of being, the self-enclosed, self-contemplating beauty of the World of Forms which is Intellect is not enough, is a very striking development of Platonism. When we bring it together in our minds, as I think we should, with that unstructured light from the Good which alone makes beauty truly beautiful, that is, lovable (above, p. 73), that light which is also life and belongs to the same kind of thought which sees the first moment in the eternal procession of Divine Intellect-Being from its source as an unstructured life which becomes structured into the World of Forms in its checked return in contemplation upon that source, the Good, then I think that we can see the opportunities which Plotinian Platonism gives for enjoying and valuing the imperfect and changing, but lively and endlessly various beauties of this earth of ours: those beauties of which Plotinus speaks so well in his great and austere late work *On Providence*:

16 P. Hadot, art. cit. p. 136.

We must conclude that the universal order is for ever something of this kind from the evidence of what we see in the All, how this order extends to everything, even to the smallest, and the art is wonderful which appears, not only in the divine beings but also in the things which one might have supposed providence would have despised for their smallness, for example the workmanship which produces wonders in rich variety in ordinary animals and the beauty of appearance which extends to the fruits and even the leaves of plants, and their beauty of flower which comes so effortlessly, and their delicacy and variety, and that all this has not been made once and come to an end but is always being made as the powers above move in different ways over this world. (III 2 [47] 13, 17-27, tr. A. H. Armstrong).

We should not interpret what has just been said as meaning to imply that there is in the thought of Plotinus any devaluation of the World of Forms. He would be a very strange kind of Platonist indeed if there was. He is indeed very conscious, as we have seen, of the transcendent pre-eminence of its source, the Good, and of the light and life which flows from it. But his celebrations of the beauty and glory of the world of real being are unsurpassed in Platonic literature, and sometimes rather startling to those who are inclined to think of the Forms in text-book Platonist terms as some kind of hypostatized abstract universals composing a cosmos of static perfection. The light which is life predominates within it, as it transcends it and extends below it. Though its unity is incomparably more unified than that of our world here below, it is the unity of a plenitude in the richest variety. It contains absolutely everything in the material cosmos, even individuals wherever their individuality is more than merely numerical and is the result of a difference which must be considered one of form.[17] Everything is there, and everything there, even what is most irrational, lifeless and inert here below, is living thought which is formed and structured life at its most intense, united with and transparent to all else and so charged with unbounded glory. A

17 On Forms of individuals in Plotinus see A. H. Armstrong "Form, Individual and Person in Plotinus", *Plotinian and Christian Studies* XX: references to other important discussions are given in n. 1.

sentence from one of Plotinus' great visionary descriptions of the
World of Forms may give an idea of how he experienced it:

> They [the Forms in Intellect] all flow, in a way, from a single spring, not like one
> particular breath or one warmth, but as if there was one quality which held and
> kept intact all the qualities in itself, of sweetness along with fragrance, and was at
> once the quality of wine and the character of all tastes, the sights of colours and
> all the awarenesses of touch, and all that hearings hear, all tunes and every
> rhythm. (VI 7 [38] 12, 23-30. tr. A. H. Armstrong).

And this intelligible cosmos, which is our material cosmos with all
its beauties intensified and seen *sub specie aeternitatis*, is most
intimately and immediately present in our world here and now.
Plotinus is particularly concerned throughout the Enneads to
bring out to the full the implications of the incorporeality of the
intelligible, and, in spite of occasional slight distortions due to the
influence of the cosmic piety discussed above (pp. 59-63), succeeds
extremely well. One of the most important is that because the
intelligible, since it is incorporeal, is not in space or time, it is
immediately present as a whole at every point in space and every
moment of time. "For the sense-world is in one place, but the
intelligible world is everywhere" (V 9 [5]) 13-14 tr. A. H. A.). This
immediacy of presence is not affected by the intermediacy of Soul.
It is Soul, not Intellect, in Plotinus which forms, governs and
animates the material cosmos, imparting to it its proper degree of
divinity: but this does not make the intelligible cosmos more
remote from the sense-world,[18] any more than the intermediacy of
the two lower hypostases makes the Good any less immediately
present to us here and now. Hierarchical superiority in the
Neoplatonists does not mean greater remoteness.

One of Plotinus' most forcible ways of expressing this immediate presence is to insist that the material cosmos is a natural, not
an artificial image. Its relation to its archetype which is also its

---

18 See V 8 [31] 7, 12-16: the chapter is one of Plotinus' frequent powerful attacks
   on the "artisan" conception of divine creation required by a literal interpretation of the *Timaeus* and shared by many Middle Platonists and most Jews and
   Christians.

creator is more like that of a shadow or a reflection to its original than that of a statue or a painting.[19] This sense of the immediate presence of archetype to image and the total continuing dependence of image on archetype which it involves is one of Plotinus' grounds for objecting to the "artisan" concept of divine creation, which requires the material cosmos to be thought of as an artefact separable and distanceable from its divine maker. The other is his strong rejection of the idea that the Divine Intellect can properly be represented as planning its creative work: its thought is not in any way discursive and its contents are not at all like the concepts with which discursive reason necessarily operates. This understanding of the nature of divine intellect, which is common to all Neoplatonists,[20] also of course helps them to apprehend the divine archetype in its material image with the vividness and directness of sense-awareness at its most intense. This understanding of the material cosmos as an image which manifests and makes present its incorporeal divine archetype on the level of body and sense is the essential of the Platonic awareness of the divine presence in and enhancement of earthly beauties. As we have seen, it was developed and intensified with great power by Plotinus. But precisely because of the strength of his presentation we become particularly aware in reading the *Enneads* of an ambiguity intrinsic to the idea of "image" in the valuation of this world here below which runs through the whole Platonic tradition, an ambiguity, perhaps, very close to the ambiguity of the cosmos itself. The concept of "image" requires, and indeed demands, a sliding scale of valuation. At the lower end of the scale the emphasis is on the difference between image and archetype and the inferiority of the former to the latter. One says "How, poor, trivial and inadequate

19 See VI 4 [22] 10. VI 4 is the first part of the great work *On The Presence of Being, One and the Same, Everywhere as a Whole*, which is of central importance for understanding this aspect of Plotinus' thought.
20 For its powerful expression by Proclus see A. H. Armstrong "The Negative Theology of *Nous* in Later Neoplatonism" in *Platonismus und Christentum* ed. H.-D. Blume u. F. Mann (Aschendorff, Münster 1983) pp. 31-37.

a thing this mere image is compared with the original". At the higher end the emphasis is not only on the excellence of the image on its proper level, "this perceptible god, image of the intelligible, greatest and best, most beautiful and most perfect", as Plato calls it in the last sentence of the *Timaeus*. It is also, most strongly in Plotinus and later Platonism, on the presence in it of the divine archetype and the light which comes from beyond. Here one is moved to use *eikōn* not in its neutral or derogatory earlier Greek sense but in the strong and sacred sense which it has come to have in the Orthodox Church. One will say "How beautiful and venerable is this icon of the eternal not made with human hands. In it we encounter the presence and power of God". There are of course many intermediate stages on this scale of valuation, and lower and higher valuations can be held together in a Platonist's mind and applied to the world together at any one time, as is generally the case with Plotinus. But when the higher valuation predominates we can see coming together the basic Platonic and Christian faith in the goodness on its own level of the divinely made material world, the awareness of that light from the Good which reaches from its source beyond the real being of the intelligible down to the lowest limits of anything which can in any way exist, and the sense of the living presence of the archetype in its natural image, to give the late Platonic understanding of this world as the icon of the divine the enduring power which it has had in our tradition.

We have not, in the modern period of the scholarly study of ancient philosophy, been inclined to take the later Neoplatonists, Iamblichus and his successors, very seriously or to read very much of the voluminous surviving works of the great Athenian Proclus, until the last two decades or so. But the revival of interest in them which has led to the publication of admirable new critical editions and a closer and more comprehensive study of the increasingly accessible texts has recently led to a much better understanding and appreciation of some parts of their thought which were ignored, or rather contemptuously dismissed, by earlier generations. One which is of particular relevance to the subject of this paper is their final total rehabilitation of the dark, material, feminine principle. The history of this "dark other" in the Pythagorean-Platonic tradition is rather complex. I have attempted to sketch it elsewhere.[21] It is generally said to be *kakon* and the cause of *kaka* here below, and this means that it is regarded with hostility and suspicion, not least by Plotinus. But we always need to remember in considering this that the "dark other" which is *kakon* is one of the two absolutely indispensable constituents of a universe which is strongly affirmed to be good and beautiful, as indispensable to its very existence as the male principle of form and light. This makes it rather risky, and at times misleading, to translate *kakon* into modern languages by words which have sinister overtones from Christian demonology, as "evil" has in English. Platonic-Pythagorean dualism is never simply a conflict-dualism of the Iranian pattern, even in those Middle Platonists like Plutarch and Atticus who stand closest to this and were perhaps influenced by it. For the greatest part of its history it occupies a strange intermediate area between dualisms of Iranian type and those which are best symbolized by the Chinese Yang-Yin circle. What the last Hellenic Neoplatonists achieve is to bring it over firmly to the "Chinese" side by giving an account of the "dark other" and its relationship to the principle of light, form and order which is perfectly in accord with the Yang-Yin circle. They see the two principles as equal in honour, proceeding directly from the ineffable One/Good which is beyond all duality and difference. They are the father and mother of all that exists, of real being and the intelligible cosmos as well as of the material cosmos. And they see them in this way without denying that the "dark other" is really dark. They take full account of, and in their own way assent

21 In "Dualism, Platonic, Gnostic and Christian", *Plotinus Amid Gnostics and Christians* ed. David T. Runia (Amsterdam, Free University Press 1984) pp. 29 to 52. This will also be published in the proceedings of the International Neoplatonic Society's conference on Neoplatonism and Gnosticism held at the University of Oklahoma in March 1984.

to, everything which was said earlier in the tradition about her being responsible for the *kaka* in our necessarily imperfect world here below. But, none the less, they see in her darkness a divine and transcendent virtue.

This complete rehabilitation of the "dark other" appears fully developed in the venerated master of Proclus, Syrianus.[22] Proclus expounds it very fully and clearly in a number of passages.[23] His account in the *Timaeus* commentary brings out well how fully he takes into account all that was said by early Pythagoreans and Platonists in depreciation of the "dark other" (In Tim. I 175 Diehl, 54C 21-24).[24] And the fuller description of the two principles in the *Platonic Theology* shows particularly well the kind of divine virtue he discerns in her.

> All unity, wholeness and community of beings and all the divine measures depend in the Primal Limit, and all division and generative making (*gonimos poiēsis*) and procession to multiplicity come to be from the Supreme Un-Boundedness. (III 8, 19-23, p. 325 Saffrey-Westerink)

It is through this supreme principle, which, as Proclus notes in the *Timaeus* commentary, the ancients rightly called "darkness" and saw as the source of all the disorder and irrationality and irregularity of this world, that the creative generosity of the Good is mediated, that unbounded life-giving power which Hadot rightly saw as the supreme value for Plotinus (above, p. 74). And this generous creativity of the Unbounded extends to the lowest frontier of all the worlds, for the *hylē,* the "dark other" of the material cosmos, is her ultimate manifestation.

This recognition of the "dark other" as one of the highest divine

---

22 See Anne D. R. Sheppard "Monad and Dyad as Cosmic Principles in Syrianus", *Soul and the Structure of Being in Late Neoplatonism* ed. H. J. Blumenthal and A. C. Lloyd (Liverpool, University Press, 1982) pp. 1-17.

23 *Elements of Theology* prop. 89-92. *In Tim.* I 54 175-176 Diehl: *In Parm.* VI 1119, 4-1123, 21. *Platonic Theology* III 7-8. See J. Trouillard *La Mystagogie de Proclos* (Paris, Les Belles Lettres 1982) pp. 245-247.

24 The passage, characteristically, occurs in an allegorical exposition of the story of Atlantis.

principles can clearly do a great deal to remove the Platonic uneasiness, still apparent in Plotinus, about the beauties of the material world and their enjoyment, up to a point. The point is that at which cosmic optimism becomes altogether too roseate, and world-affirmation too easy-going and self-indulgent, and there is no longer any call to rise to the higher world of spirit. The doctrine of the Athenian Neoplatonists does not deny the evils of the material world: it is fully compatible with the austere morality of detachment from the "goods men fight about" of which I spoke earlier (pp. 70-72), and it still preserves something of the ambiguity of valuation inherent in the concept of "image" (above, pp. 76-78). But the image is now very much an icon. It becomes more necessary than ever before for the devout philosopher to be aware of the divine in and through material things and outward observances. The theory and practice of theurgy in the late Neoplatonists has recently received extensive reappraisal and is nowadays much more positively regarded by many students. In fact, though I have done what I could to help and encourage this from the beginning, I am now somewhat inclined to feel that the pendulum may have swung too far, and that we again need some of the vigorous good sense of E. R. Dodds to redress the balance. But of course these last Neo-Platonists of Athens did not only practice and commend their own theurgic Chaldaean rites. They were champions of all the old Hellenic pieties and the traditional theophanies of all mankind in a world which had officially abandoned them. All the old neglected and ruinous shrines were still full of divine presences for them. Proclus heard Athena telling him that she was coming to live in his house when the Christians turned her out of the Parthenon.[25] He thought that a philosopher should be "the hierophant of the whole world".[26] So in the history of Hellenic and Platonic awareness of the divine in the beauties of earth the beginning was present in the end. The last defenders of the primaeval theophanies were Platonic philosophers.

25 Marinus, *Life of Proclus* 30.
26 Ibid. 19.

Aphrodite, Art and Love Inspired by Beauty

The Homeric Hymns
Charles Boer, tr.

Since 1972, this version of the *Homeric Hymns*—nominated for the National Book Award—has been acclaimed by critics and public and has widely established itself as a classroom text. These thirty-five poems are the earliest extant depiction of the Gods and Goddesses as individual figures. Boer's translation is a fresh and stunning experience, offering immediate access to the archetypal characters of the Greek pantheon. Revised edition.

vi, 182 pp.   ISBN 210-0

Goddesses of Sun and Moon
Karl Kerényi

Karl Kerenyi, a colleague of C. G. Jung's and one of the major mythographers of this century, here takes a novel look at four unusual feminine configurations depicted in Greek mythology. The vision that emerges restores passionate feminine consciousness to its rightful place both in politics and in the economy of the psyche. The four papers explore the mythemes of Circe, the enchantress; Medea, the murderess; Aphrodite, the golden one; and Niobe of the Moon. Together they lend a deep psychological orientation to some of the most puzzling and controversial issues of our day: feminism, the occult, aesthetics, madness, dreams, even terrorism. Lucid, intuitive, and psychologically useful. Dunquin Series 11.

84 pp.   ISBN 211-9

Pagan Meditations
Ginette Paris

An appreciation of three Greek Goddesses as values of importance to our twentieth-century collective life: Aphrodite as civilized sexuality and beauty; Artemis as solitude, ecological significance, and a perspective on abortion; and Hestia as warm hearth, security, and stability. As the author's contribution to *imaginative* feminism, this book addresses both the meditative interior of each person and the community of culture.

204 pp.   ISBN 330-1

Rosegarden and Labyrinth
Seonaid M. Robertson

With astonishing care and precision, and aided by years of practical experience, Seonaid Robertson here explores the relationship between art and psyche. Focusing on the drawings of children and adolescents, she views these first products of the imagination against the background of artistic and cultural history. Includes drawings and photographs. Indexed.

xxix, 216 pp.   ISBN 319-0

Commentary on Plato's Symposium on Love
Marsilio Ficino, trans. Sears Jayne

Marsilio Ficino, the head of the Platonic Academy in Renaissance Florence and the first ever to translate the complete works of Plato, also wrote this Latin essay on love. Popular in European court-circles for almost two hundred years, this book influenced painters such as Botticelli and Michelangelo, and writers such as Spenser and Castiglione. Jayne's English translation, based on Marcel's edition, includes an introduction and comprehensive bibliography.

213 pp.   ISBN 601-7

Spring Publications • P.O. Box 222069 • Dallas, Texas 75222